ISBN 978-0-483-29157-7

PIBN 11294498

1 MONTH OF
FREE
READING

at

www.ForgottenBooks.com

By purchasing this book you are eligible for one month membership to ForgottenBooks.com, giving you unlimited access to our entire collection of over 1,000,000 titles via our web site and mobile apps.

To claim your free month visit:

www.forgottenbooks.com/free1294498

English
Français
Deutsche
Italiano
Español
Português

www.forgottenbooks.com

Mythology Photography **Fiction**
Fishing Christianity **Art** Cooking
Essays Buddhism Freemasonry
Medicine **Biology** Music **Ancient
Egypt** Evolution Carpentry Physics
Dance Geology **Mathematics** Fitness
Shakespeare **Folklore** Yoga Marketing
Confidence Immortality Biographies
Poetry **Psychology** Witchcraft
Electronics Chemistry History **Law**
Accounting **Philosophy** Anthropology
Alchemy Drama Quantum Mechanics
Atheism Sexual Health **Ancient History**
Entrepreneurship Languages Sport
Paleontology Needlework Islam
Metaphysics Investment Archaeology
Parenting Statistics Criminology
Motivational

SALE No. 34, JUNE 14-15, 1933

ABRAHAM LINCOLN

Books and Pamphlets, Medals,
Portraits and Autographs

The Collection Made by

JOHN SCRIPPS LITTLE

of Rushville, Ill.

Sold by Order of John L. Scripps,
of Peoria, Ill.

Unrestricted Public Auction

June 14th and 15th at 8 p. m.

CHICAGO BOOK AND ART AUCTIONS, INC.

410 SOUTH MICHIGAN AVENUE

- 9th Floor -

FOREWORD

IN 1860 John Locke Scripps wrote his famous Campaign biography of Abraham Lincoln that was published simultaneously in Chicago and New York. Lincoln heartily approved of this biography, and it was read by thousands of voters. The home of the Scripps family was Rushville, Illinois, and they knew Lincoln as a fellow-citizen who occasionally came to Rushville. It is particularly pleasant to reflect, therefore, that John Scripps Little, a nephew of this John L. Scripps, friend of Lincoln, should continue the family tradition and gather one of the finest Lincoln collections that has ever been made. It is a fitting honor to Mr. Little that his treasures are now made available to admirers of Abraham Lincoln.

Mr. Little has been a most discriminating collector. His choices have been tempered with the instinctive sense that reveals the connoisseur. First, he has kept a sharp eye to condition; he has selected only the finest copies he could get. Whitney's "Life on the Circuit," for example, is immaculate in the original jacket, as if it had come from the publishers but yesterday. And Herndon's "Lincoln" is as clean as if it had never been opened. Fine condition characterizes the library throughout.

Second, he has felt instinctively the tremendous pull of "association" items, and his collection is replete with presentation copies and relevant autograph letters. Fortunately Mr. Little is an "old hand" at the game; he has gone through all the important Lincoln sales, and added to his library choice items from them all. Consequently, many of his books are pedigreed; they have valuable histories from the famous Hart, Burton, Lambert and McAleenan Collections. Most of the pamphlets were presented by the authors to Charles H. Hart and later acquired by Major Lambert.

Unfortunately Major Lambert's library was endangered by fire; so that a few of the pamphlets are partly damp-stained, but this merely guarantees their authenticity. Practically all of Major Lambert's pamphlets are finely bound in three-quarter green morocco, marbled boards, and except for the occasional damp-stains, in excellent condition. In each instance the original wrappers have been bound in; so that this fact has not been repeated throughout the catalogue. To aid in cataloguing, the abbreviation A.P.C. has been used for Autograph Presentation Copy, in addition to the usual A.L.S. for Autograph Letter Signed, T.L.S. for Typed Letter Signed and A.MS.S. for Autograph Manuscript Signed.

This is one of the most comprehensive Lincoln collections offered for public sale since the disposal of the famous Lambert collection in 1914. And, what is more startling, it may be the last, since the two great private collections now' in existence will probably go to public institutions. The dispersal of Mr. Little's library brings to light new bibliographical information and furnishes mature guidance to the whole range of Lincolniana. The new collector may be lead to significant material, and the experienced collector may be stirred with the joy of appreciating rare books and their associations.

Franklin J. Meine

SALE NO. 34

ABRAHAM LINCOLN

Rare pamphlets, books, autograph letters,
portraits and prints

Fine association items from the Hart,
Burton and Lambert Collections

Sale Wednesday and Thursday

June 14-15, at 8 p. m.

Free Public Exhibit

beginning
Saturday, June 3, to 14
9 a. m. to 9 p. m.
daily except Sunday
Ninth Floor

CHICAGO BOOK & ART AUCTIONS, INC.

410 SOUTH MICHIGAN AVENUE

CHICAGO, ILLINOIS

CONDITIONS OF SALE

1. This sale is conducted by Chicago Book & Art Auctions, Inc.; and the Directors reserve the right to determine upon any conditions or circumstances attending the sale.

2. All bids are to be so much *per lot* as numbered in the catalogue.

3. Terms cash. A cash deposit of 25% shall be made at the time of sale, if requested.

4. Title passes upon the fall of the auctioneer's hammer, and thereafter the property is entirely at the purchaser's risk. All articles must be called for the following day from 1 to 6 P. M., Room 919 Fine Arts Building. For all out-of-town shipments an extra charge will be made to cover packing and shipping. Articles not called for the following day, or not paid for in full, may at the option of the firm be re-sold.

5. All books are sold as catalogued and are assumed to be in good second-hand condition. If critical defects are found, not mentioned in the catalogue, the lot may be returned, provided that notice of such defects is given promptly and the goods returned within seven days after the sale. *Magazines and other periodicals, also miscellaneous lots of books arranged in parcels, are sold as they are, without recourse.*

6. Autograph letters, documents, manuscripts, inscriptions in books, etc., are sold as catalogued and without recourse. The firm will make every effort to determine the authenticity and genuineness of all such material and to describe it correctly, but it can not be absolutely guaranteed.

7. All bids, whether manual, oral, or by written request are made subject to the above Conditions of Sale.

FIRST SESSION
Wednesday Evening, June 14, 8 p.m.

BOOKS AND PAMPHLETS, NOS. 1 TO 380

1. **ABOTT, A. ABOTT.** The Assassination and Death of Abraham Lincoln. New York, American News Company, 1865. 12mo, half calf. First edition. (12pp. of text) Rare. Fish 3.

2. **ADAMS, GEORGE E.** Lincoln, Address Delivered at Quincy, Illinois, October 13, 1908, etc. Peterboro, N. H., 1908. 8vo, three-quarter morocco, boards. Oakleaf 5.

3. **ADDRESSES AND SERMONS.** A Collection of seventeen Addresses and Sermons by H. A. Boardman (1000), A. H. Bullock (2500), C. B. Crane, H. C. Deming (3500), John Fowler (930), Newman Hall, J. G. Holland (5000), J. McClintock (2500), A. D. Mayo (1000), W. F. Paddock (2000), J. W. Patterson (Autographed), Matthew Simpson (2000) two copies, R. S. Storrs (1500), Union League, Philadelphia, E. N. White, (1000), R. B. Yard (800). Various sizes, original wrappers. Fish 109, 151, 231, 257, 329, 375, 425, 616, 646, 726, 733, 859, 907, 984, 1038, and 1074 respectively.

4. **ALLEN, ETHAN.** A Discourse . . . on the Murder of our late President. Baltimore, 1865. 12mo, unbound. 300 copies. Fish 25.

5. **ALLEN, LYMAN WHITNEY.** Abraham Lincoln, A Poem. New York, 1896. 12mo, original cloth, gilt top.
First edition. Extra-illustrated with 36 portraits, many India proofs, two of which, the frontispiece and the one opposite page 15 are limited to 50 proofs, etched by Charles B. Hall. Also many exquisite vignettes and head and tail pieces. Burton collection. Fish 27.

6. **ALLEN, LYMAN WHITNEY.** Abraham Lincoln, A Poem. New York, 1896. 12mo, cloth, gilt top.
Second edition. A.P.C. to Thomas Nast. A.L.S. by Allen to Nast, 4to, 2 pages, Aug. 10th, 1896; asking him to illustrate his "Abraham Lincoln," giving references, etc. A.L.S. by Nast, 12mo, one page Sept. 1, 1888; sending some drawings to The Graphic Co. Also laid in are signature of Nast, clipping of Allen and book plate of J. S. Little. Fish 27.

7. **ANDREW, JOHN A.** Address to the Legislature of Massachusetts. Boston, 1864. A.L.S. and photograph, autographed. ✛**SUMNER, CHARLES.** The Promises of the Declaration of Independence. Boston, 1865. A.L.S. Fish 914. Together two pamphlets, 8vo, original wrappers.

[5]

8. ANGLE, PAUL M. LINCOLN IN THE YEARS 1854, 1855, 1856, 1857, 1860, Being the Day-by-Day Activities of Lincoln. Springfield, The Lincoln Centennial Association, (1928-30). Together five pamphlets, 8vo, original wrappers. First printings.

9. ARNAUD, ACHILLE. ABRAHAM LINCOLN, Sa Naissance, Sa Vie, Sa Mort. [*Illustrated*] Paris, 1865. 4to, half morocco. Fish 33.

10. ARNOLD, ISAAC N. RECONSTRUCTION: Liberty the Cornerstone, and Lincoln the Architect. Washington, 1864. 8vo, three-quarter calf. First edition. Burton collection. Fish 34.

11. ARNOLD, ISAAC N. SKETCH OF THE LIFE OF ABRAHAM LINCOLN. New York, 1869. Unbound. ✛THE LIFE OF ABRAHAM LINCOLN. Chicago, 1885. Cloth. ✛THE HISTORY OF ABRAHAM LINCOLN AND THE OVERTHROW OF SLAVERY. Chicago, 1867. Three-quarter calf; rubbed. Together three volumes, 8vo.
First editions of first two. 2 A.L.S. by Arnold laid in. First mentioned designed to accompany engraving of Chappel's painting, "The Last Hours of Lincoln." Fish 36, 41, 35.

12. ARNOLD, ISAAC N. CHICAGO HISTORICAL SOCIETY. Address, Giving a History of the Society and its Acquisitions . . . with Incidents in the Lives of Abraham Lincoln and Major Anderson, etc. Chicago, 1877. 8vo, three-quarter morocco. A.P.C. Not in Fish or Oakleaf.

13. ARNOLD, ISAAC N. REMINISCENCES OF LINCOLN AND CONGRESS During the Rebellion, New York Genealogical and Biographical Record. New York, July 1882. 4to, three-quarter straight grained calf. A.P.C. by Arnold to Hart, and A.P.C. by Hart to Lambert. Not in Fish or Oakleaf.

WITH A SEPARATE VOLUME OF EXTRA ILLUSTRATIONS AND AUTOGRAPHS

14. ARNOLD, ISAAC N. THE LIFE OF ABRAHAM LINCOLN. Chicago, 1885. Each leaf inlaid to 4to; with volume of extra plates and autographs all inlaid or mounted to 4to. Together two volumes, blue morocco, gilt tooled, gilt tops, moiré silk doublures and end papers. Fish 41.
First edition. The extra illustrations include circa 90 fine portraits and 85 autographs. The many important autographs cover not only the years of Lincoln's life, but go back to the beginning of the Republic. They include an autograph endorsement, signed by Benjamin Franklin, 6 lines, March 13, 1787; an A.D. by Lincoln, 1839, legal affidavit; a leaf of A.MS. by John Brown of Osawatomie; a fine A.L.S. "Ulysses" from Gen. Grant to his father, Sept. 19, 1865; and A.L.S. by Beauregard, H. W. Beecher, E. Bates, J. P. Benjamin, J. C. Breckenridge, H. Clay, C. A. Dana, J. Davis, S. A. Douglas, S. Cameron, H. Greeley, W. Scott, W. H. Seward, W. T. Sherman, D. Webster and others.

EXTRA-ILLUSTRATED

15. ARNOLD, ISAAC N. THE LIFE OF ABRAHAM LINCOLN. Two volumes. Chicago, 1885. Large 8vo, three-quarter red morocco, boards, gilt tops. Fish 41.
First edition. The original volume extended to two by the insertion of a specially printed title page and about 108 engravings of the leaders in the government and

Civil War. A.L.S. laid in referring to Benedict Arnold, and 2 A.L.S. by Hon. E. B. Washburn, the writer of the Introduction. Magnificent set.

16. ASSASSINATION. THE TERRIBLE TRAGEDY AT WASHINGTON. Assassination of President Lincoln. Last Hours and Death-Bed Scenes . . . A Full and Graphic Account of this Great National Calamity, etc. *A correct likeness of all the parties in any way connected with the lamentable event.* Philadelphia, [1865]. 8vo, three-quarter morocco. Book plate of Gov. Pennypacker. Fish 937.

17. ASSASSINATION. TRIAL OF THE CONSPIRATORS. Argument of John A. Bingham. Washington, 1865. ✛ OPINION . . . by James Speed. Washington, 1865. ✛ REMINISCENCES . . . OF THE ASSASSINATION OF LINCOLN. By J. E. Buckingham. Washington, 1894. Together three pamphlets, 8vo, wrappers. Fish 93, 878 and 147.

18. ASSASSINATION. APPENDIX TO DIPLOMATIC CORRESPONDENCE OF 1865. The Assassination of Abraham Lincoln. Washington, 1866. 8vo, half morocco, boards. Not in Fish or Oakleaf.

19. ASSOCIATION, LINCOLN CENTENNIAL, (SPRING-FIELD). A Collection of eleven Addresses, Announcements, Bulletins, Menus, etc. With T.L.S. re society. Oakleaf 65, 68, 69, 75, 79, 80 and 84.

20. ATWOOD, E. S. IN MEMORIAM. [I] The Nation's Loss. [II] The President's Record. Salem, 1865. 8vo, three-quarter morocco. 500 copies. A.L.S. to Hart re book. Hart, Lambert copy. Fish 47.

RARE PRESENTATION COPY

21. BANCROFT, GEORGE. MEMORIAL ADDRESS ON THE LIFE AND CHARACTER OF ABRAHAM LINCOLN. [*Engraved portrait*] Washington, 1866. 8vo, original cloth.

First edition. A.P.C. on fly leaf: "Mrs. Sarah J. Boerum Wetmore, from her Friend the Author of the Address, Geo. Bancroft. Newport, Aug., 1866." Any presentation copies from Bancroft are particularly rare. Major Wetmore was in command of the police arrangements at Lincoln's funeral. A.L.S. by Bancroft, 8vo, one page, laid in, N.Y., 12 April 1866, referring to the publication of the Address. Fish 61.

22. BALDRIDGE, S. C. THE MARTYR PRINCE. A Sermon, etc. at Friendsville, Ill. Cincinnati, 1865. 8vo, three-quarter morocco. 500 copies. A.L.S. to Hart, sending names of three other sermons on Lincoln. Hart, Lambert copy. Fish 55.

23. (BARKER, H. E.) LINCOLN AND DOUGLAS. A Broadside published 1866 by Wm. H. Herndon. ✛ A CARD AND A CORRECTION. Nov. 9, 1882. ✛ LINCOLN'S MARRIAGE. Newspaper Interview with Mrs. Frances Wallace. Sept. 2, 1895. ✛ MARY LINCOLN. A Letter to her Cousin, Elizabeth Todd Grimsly. Sept. 29, 1861. Together four pamphlets, 8vo, printed wrappers; privately printed by H. E. Barker, 1917. Limited to 75 copies each, signed. Oakleaf 620, 619, 1448.

24. (BARKER, H. E.) OLD SALEM CHAUTAUQUA. Petersburg, Ill., 1900. 8vo, half cloth. Poem and A.N.S. by Barker on p. 47.

25. BARNARD, D. D. TRUTH FOR THE TIMES . . . Why no Friend of the Union can be a Republican, etc. St. Louis, [1860]. 8vo, unbound, 8 leaves; lightly foxed. Lambert sale, no. 44. Not in Fish or Oakleaf.

26. BARNES, ALBERT. THE STATE OF THE COUNTRY. Philadelphia, 1865. 8vo, three-quarter morocco. 500 printed. A.P.C. Burton collection. Fish 67.

27. BARRETT, FRANK W. Z. MOURNING FOR LINCOLN. Philadelphia, 1909. 12mo, original cloth, gilt top.
First edition. A.P.C. to Maj. Lambert and T.L.S. presenting the book, and A.L. of Maj. Lambert's reply laid in. Oakleaf 105.

28. BARTLETT, D. W. THE LIFE AND PUBLIC SERVICES OF HON. ABRAHAM LINCOLN. New York, Derby & Jackson, 1860. 12mo, original wrappers; back wrapper loose. First edition. Fish 75.

29. BARTON, WILLIAM E. THE LIFE OF ABRAHAM LINCOLN. *Illustrated.* Two volumes. Indianapolis, (1925). 8vo, original cloth, gilt tops, jackets, boxed.
Limited edition for subscribers, signed. A.L.S. by Mary Rennels, referring to set, laid in. Oakleaf 133.

30. BARTON, WILLIAM E. THE LIFE OF ABRAHAM LINCOLN. *Illustrated.* Two volumes. Indianapolis, (1925). 8vo, three-quarter blue morocco, marbled boards, gilt tops.
First edition. A.P.C. on sheet and autograph laid in. Fine set. Oakleaf 133.

31. BATES, DAVID HOMER. LINCOLN IN THE TELEGRAPH OFFICE. [Excerpts from the Century Magazine, 1907] Large 8vo, three-quarter morocco. Two T.L.S. re book, one to Maj. Lambert. Lambert copy.

32. BEIDLER, J. H. LINCOLN; or, the Prime Hero of the Nineteenth Century. Chicago, 1896. Square 12mo, original cloth.
First edition. Very scarce. 2 A.L.S. by Beidler to E. C. Stedman tipped in, with Stedman's book plate. Fish 83.

33. BENJAMIN, S. G. W. ODE ON THE DEATH OF ABRAHAM LINCOLN. Boston, 1865. 12mo, wrappers. 250 copies. Fish 89.

34. BEVERIDGE, ALBERT J. ABRAHAM LINCOLN, 1809-1858. *With illustrations.* Four volumes. Boston, 1928. 4to, half buckram, boards, paper labels.
Limited to 1000 sets of the Manuscript edition. Four A.L.S. by Beveridge to his secretary, Edward H. Bohne, written while he was composing the work, Chicago, July 3, 1925; N. Y., Dec. 16, 1925; Beverly Farms, Mass., Jan. 4, 1927; N. Y., Jan. 7, 1927; and a T.L.S., Beverly Farms, Oct. 7, 1925. All refer to his biography.

35. BEVERIDGE, ALBERT J. ABRAHAM LINCOLN. [*Illustrated*] Two volumes. Boston, 1928. Large 8vo, cloth, jackets, boxed.
First edition. A.L.S. by Beveridge to Mr. Little who supplied a photograph of the Rushville Court House where Lincoln tried cases. Fine set.

36. BINGHAM, JOEL F. National Disappointment. Buffalo, 1865. 8vo, three-quarter morocco. 500 copies. A.P.C. to R. B. Potts. Biography of author inside front cover by W. J. Potts. Fish 92.

37. BINNEY, WILLIAM. Proceedings of the City Council of Providence on the Death of President Lincoln: with the Oration. Providence, 1865. Narrow 4to, three-quarter morocco. 500 copies of this large paper edition. A.L.S. detailing editions. Lambert copy. Fish 94.

38. BIOGRAPHICAL SKETCHES. A Collection of six pamphlets by H. C. McCook, L. G. Marsh, Wm. H. Lambert, G. F. Tracy (T.L.S. to Lambert), F. H. Wines (A.P.C.), and Morris Sheppard (A.L.S. to Lambert). All 8vo, three-quarter morocco. Fish 622, 637, 782, 962, 1066 and Oakleaf 1275.

39. BIOGRAPHY. The Life and Public Services of Abraham Lincoln. By Henry J. Raymond. *Illustrated.* New York, 1865. ✝The Life of Abraham Lincoln. By J. G. Holland. Springfield, Mass., 1866. ✝Abraham Lincoln. By Mrs. P. A. Hanaford. Boston, 1865. ✝Abraham Lincoln. By William O. Stoddard. *With illustrations.* New York, 1884. Together four volumes, 8vo, cloth.
First editions. A.L.S. by Raymond and 2 by Holland laid in first two mentioned. Fish 791, 426, 384, 899.

40. BIOGRAPHY. A Glimpse of the U. S. Telegraph Corps. By Wm. B. Wilson. (1889) A.P.C. Fish 1063. ✝Abraham Lincoln on Waterways. By W. A. Meese. 1908. A.P.C. and A.L.S. Oakleaf 953. ✝Lincoln in the Black Hawk War. By A. A. Jackson. 1898. Lambert copy. ✝Loyal Publication Society. No. 4. "The Three Voices." 1863. ✝Curiosities of the Lincoln Cult. By A. S. Chapman. Excerpt. Together five volumes, 8vo, half calf and three-quarter morocco.

41. BIOGRAPHY. Abraham Lincoln. By Eugene C. Allen. Albion, Mich., 1895. Fish 26. ✝Abraham Lincoln. By Frederick W. Lehmann. St. Louis, 1908. A.P.C. to Lambert. Oakleaf 806. ✝Lincoln. By James A. Connoly. Peoria, 1910. 4 leaves. Autographed. Oakleaf 381. ✝The Solitude of Abraham Lincoln. By E. J. Edwards. Putnam, Conn., 1916. Limited to 30 copies, signed. Oakleaf 475. Together four pamphlets, original wrappers.

42. BIOGRAPHY. A Collection of nine volumes by W. E. Curtis, Henry Ketcham, Chas. Minor, I. N. Phillips, J. C. Power, M. R. S. Andrews, H. Barrett, H. B. Binns and I. N. Phillips. 1889-1910. Fish 240, 486, 654, 748 (1st issue), 765 (Autographed by A. S. Edwards, nephew of Lincoln) ; Oakleaf 27, 106, 158 and 1103 (A.P.C. to Lambert).

43. BIOGRAPHY. A Collection of ten volumes, nine titles, by O. L. Barler, J. T. Morse, E. L. Staples, M. R. S. Andrews, E. W. Chafin,

J. Jennings, O. Roberts and W. Wayne (Not in Oakleaf). 1893-1918. Fish 66 (2 copies), 666, 888; Oakleaf 27, 327 (A.P.C. to Lambert), 741, 1188 (Large paper, signed); and "The Life . . . of Abraham Lincoln," Boston, 1860.

44. BIRD, M. B. THE VICTORIOUS, A Small Poem on the Assassination of President Lincoln. By M. B. Bird, Wesleyan Missionary, Port-au-Prince, Hayti. M. DeCordova, McDougall & Co., Booksellers, Stationers, and Publishers, Kingston, Jamaica, 1866. 12mo, original cloth; small stain on front cover. First edition. Rare. Fish 97.

45. BLAIR, MONTGOMERY. COMMENTS ON THE POLICY INAUGURATED BY THE PRESIDENT. New York, 1863. 8vo, three-quarter morocco. A.L.S. and extra autograph. Burton collection. Fish 101.

46. BLISS, T. E. A DISCOURSE Commemorative of the Life and Character of Abraham Lincoln. Memphis, Tenn., 1865. Two copies, 8vo, three-quarter morocco and half calf. 1000 copies. A.P.C. Hart, Lambert copy. Fish 106.

47. BOARDMAN, GEORGE N. THE DEATH OF PRESIDENT LINCOLN. Binghamton, N. Y., 1865. 8vo, three-quarter morocco. 500 copies. Two A.L.S. to Hart re book. Hart, Lambert copy. Fish 108.

48. BOKER, GEORGE H. OUR HEROIC THEMES, A Poem Read before the Phi Beta Kappa Society of Harvard University. Boston, 1865. 16mo, half cloth. A.L.S. to A. Boyd. Boyd, Lambert copy. Not in Fish or Oakleaf.

49. (BOOTH, JOHN WILKES) ESCAPE AND SUICIDE OF JOHN WILKES BOOTH, Assassin of President Lincoln. By Finis L. Bates. Memphis, 1907. 12mo, original cloth.
First edition. First issue: with entire first paragraph misprinted on page 9, begins "of slavery" and ends "by law." Only a few copies so printed. A.P.C., inscribed on fly leaf: "To John E. Burton with compliments of the Author, this book, one of the first copies published. Finis L. Bates." Extra-illustrated by the insertion of about 25 photographs and clippings, one of which states that the body of Booth was mummified, and owned by an undertaker of Enid, Okla. Oakleaf 136.

50. BOOTH, ROBERT RUSSELL. PERSONAL FORGIVENESS AND PUBLIC JUSTICE. New York, 1865. 8vo, three-quarter morocco. 1000 copies. A.L.S. to Hart re book. Hart, Lambert copy. Fish 116.

51. BOUTWELL, GEORGE S. EULOGY ON THE DEATH OF ABRAHAM LINCOLN. Lowell [Mass.], 1865. 8vo, half calf. 1000 copies. A.L.S. Fish 124.

LARGE PAPER COPY

52. BOYD, ANDREW. A MEMORIAL LINCOLN BIBLIOGRAPHY: Being an Account of Books, Eulogies, Sermons, Portraits, Engravings,

Medals, etc. published upon Abraham Lincoln. Albany, N. Y., 1870. Large 4to, three-quarter morocco, marbled boards, leather labels.
Limited to 250 copies; one of a few printed on large paper. Introduction by the famous collector, C. H. Hart. Burton collection. Fish 126.

53. BOYD, ANDREW. ABRAHAM LINCOLN, Foully Assassinated . . . A Poem with an Illustration, from the London Punch, for May 6, 1865. Albany, N. Y., Joel Munsel, 1868. 4to, 5 unbound signatures.
Limited to 75 copies. Handsomely printed on alternate pages. Fish 125.

54. BOYD, L[UCINDA]. THE SORROWS OF NANCY. Richmond, Va., O. E. Flanhart Printing Company, 1899. 12mo, original cloth.
First edition. Superb copy. Fish says: "Lucinda had notions about Lincoln's parentage." Laid in are two newspaper clippings, The Courier Journal, Louisville, Ky., June 17th, 1906, giving memorial exercises and claims to Lincoln's birthplace. Fish 127.

55. BOYHOOD BIOGRAPHY. THE FOREST BOY. By Z. A. Mudge. *Four illustrations.* New York, (1867). 12mo; rubbed, soiled. ✚IN THE BOYHOOD OF LINCOLN. By Hezekiah Butterworth. New York, 1892. 8vo. ✚CHOOSING "ABE" LINCOLN CAPTAIN. *Illustrated.* New York, 1899. 12mo. ✚ABRAHAM LINCOLN CENTENNIAL. By Lilian C. Bergold. New York, (1908). 8vo. ✚THE PIONEER BOY. By William M. Thayer. Boston, 1863. 12mo; rubbed. Together five volumes, original cloth.
First editions of first four. Very fine copies, save for defects noted. Fish 669, 166, 199; Oakleaf 150 (A.P.C.); Fish 941 (Sixth Thousand).

56. BRIGGS, GEORGE W. EULOGY ON ABRAHAM LINCOLN. Salem, Mass., 1865. 4to, original wrappers; slightly rubbed. Limited edition on large paper. Fish 134.

57. BROADSIDE. JOURNAL & COURIER—EXTRA. Death of President Lincoln. Condition of Secretary Seward. The Plot Discovered. The Assassins Known! Narrow folio, 1p.

58. BROADSIDES. THREE COPPERHEAD BROADSIDES. Folio, 1p. each. Controversial articles.

59. BROADSIDES. A Collection of six Broadsides, The Nation's Exultation Turned to Mourning, Sheridan's Ride!, A Singular Dream, The Duty of the Colored Voter, etc.

60. BROSS, WILLIAM. HISTORY OF CHICAGO. What I Remember of Early Chicago. Chicago, 1876. 8vo, original cloth.
First edition. A.L.S. by Bross, 8vo, 3 pages, laid in; To His Excellency, Abraham Lincoln, Springfield, 1865. Soliciting an appointment. Bross was Lt. Governor of Illinois.

61. (BROWNING, ORVILLE H.) THE DIARY OF ORVILLE HICKMAN BROWNING. Edited by T. C. Pease and J. G. Randall. Springfield, Ill., 1925. Thick 8vo, cloth.
A.L.S. by Browning to Lincoln, "Quincy, Ills. Sept. 27, 1861;" recommending James Simpson for a judicial appointment. And two A.D.S., 1867, one to Andrew Boyd. So friendly was Lincoln with the family that he could write Mrs. Browning of his unsuccessful love affairs. Oakleaf 1089.

62. BURRAGE, HENRY S. GETTYSBURG AND LINCOLN. *Illustrated.* New York, 1906. 8vo, cloth, gilt top, jacket. First edition. Oakleaf 234.

63. BURTON, JOHN E. ABRAHAM LINCOLN, An Oration. 1903. Two copies, 4to. ✠ABRAHAM LINCOLN. By W. W. Whitcombe. Milwaukee, John E. Burton, 1905. 8vo. Together three pamphlets, wrappers.
Limited to 26 on tinted paper, 150 and 26 copies, respectively, each signed. Fish 161 and Oakleaf 1485.

64. BUTLER, C. M. FUNERAL ADDRESS. Philadelphia, 1865. 8vo, wrappers. 750 copies. A.L.S. Fish 163.

65. BUTLER, J. G. THE MARTYR PRESIDENT. Our Grief and Our Duty. Washington, 1865. Two copies bound in 8vo, three-quarter morocco. A.L.S. Burton collection. Fish 165.

66. CAMPAIGN OF 1860. WELLS' ILLUSTRATED NATIONAL HAND-BOOK FOR 1860. *57 illustrations.* New York, 1860. 12mo. ✠A POLITICAL TEXT-BOOK FOR 1860. Compiled by Horace Greeley and John P. Cleveland. New York, 1860. 8vo. ✠LINCOLN'S CAMPAIGN. By Osborn H. Oldroyd. *Profusely illustrated.* Chicago, (1896). 12mo. Together three volumes, original cloth.
First editions. First mentioned very scarce. Fish 1032, 361 and 712.

67. CAREY, [ISAAC E.] ABRAHAM LINCOLN, the Value to the Nation of his Exalted Character. Freeport, Ill., 1865. 8vo, three-quarter morocco. Rare. Lambert copy. Fish 175.

68. CARMICHAEL, ORTON H. TYPED MANUSCRIPT. "Lincoln's Gettysburg Address." *With proofs of photographs.* 4to, 81 pages. ✠LINCOLN'S GETTYSBURG ADDRESS. [*Illustrated*] New York, (1917). 12mo, original cloth, jacket. Together two pieces.
The original printer's copy with innumerable autograph corrections, together with the first edition of the book, autographed on the fly leaf. Oakleaf 255.

69. CARNAHAN, D. T. ORATION ON THE DEATH OF ABRAHAM LINCOLN. Gettysburg, 1865. Two copies, 8vo, half calf. 500 copies. A.P.C. and A.L.S. re book: "The edition is entirely exhausted and I have not a copy." Fish 176.

70. CARPENTER, F. B. THE INNER LIFE OF LINCOLN. Six Months at the White House. New York, 1870. ✠THE PICTURE AND THE MEN: Together with the Life of the Celebrated Artist, F. B. Carpenter, etc. Compiled by Fred. B. Perkins. [*Engraved portrait of Carpenter*] New York, 1867. Together two volumes, 12mo, original cloth.
A.P.C. of first mentioned to Thomas Nast from Carpenter, who painted the large historical picture of Lincoln signing the Emancipation Proclamation. First edition of second mentioned. Very fine copies. Fish 177 and 745.

71. CARR, CLARK E. LINCOLN AT GETTYSBURG. *Illustrated.* Chicago, 1906. Two copies, tall 16mo, cloth. First edition of first. Both autographed. Oakleaf 258.

72. CATON, JOHN DEAN. EARLY BENCH AND BAR OF ILLINOIS. [*Illustrated with portraits*] Chicago, 1893. 8vo, original cloth. *First edition. Contains much material re Lincoln. Superb copy. Not in Fish or Oakleaf.*

73. CENTENARY OF 1909. THE CENTENARY OF THE BIRTH OF ABRAHAM LINCOLN. Washington, O. H. Oldroyd, 1908. Two copies, one first edition. Oakleaf 1072. ✛ONE HUNDREDTH ANNIVERSARY. Baptist Temple. Philadelphia, 1909. Oakleaf 301. ✛THE LAW ASSOCIATION OF PHILADELPHIA. 1909. Oakleaf 301. ✛LINCOLN CENTENNIAL. (Springfield), 1909. Three-quarter morocco. Together five volumes, 8vo, first four in original wrappers.

74. CHAMBERLAIN, JOSHUA L. ABRAHAM LINCOLN, Seen from the Field in the War for the Union. [Privately printed], 1909. 8vo, three-quarter morocco. A.P.C. and A.L.S. to Lambert. Oakleaf 328.

75. CHAMBERLAIN, N. H. THE ASSASSINATION OF PRESIDENT LINCOLN. 16mo, wrappers. 500 copies. Fish 186.

76. [CHASE, SALMON P.] MEMORIAL RECORD OF THE NATION'S TRIBUTE TO ABRAHAM LINCOLN. Compiled by B. F. Morris. Washington, 1865. 8vo, morocco, gilt edges, gilt lettered: "Hon. Salmon P. Chase, Chief Justice U. S." *Chief Justice Chase's own copy with his autograph signature pasted on fly leaf. Fish 665.*

77. CHICAGO. CHICAGO TRIBUNE CAMPAIGN DOCUMENT, No. 1. Spirit of the Chicago Convention. Extracts from all the notable speeches delivered in and out of the National "Democratic" Convention. [1864] 8vo, unbound, stitched, 8 leaves. Rare. Not in Fish or Oakleaf. Original of Fish 190.

78. CHICAGO. CHICAGO TRIBUNE CAMPAIGN DOCUMENT, No. 2. Issues of the Campaign. Shall the North Vote for a Disunion Peace. [1864] 8vo, three-quarter morocco. Burton collection. Not in Fish or Oakleaf.

79. CIVIL WAR. "BLACKWOOD'S" HISTORY OF THE UNITED STATES. By F. S. Dickson. 1896. A.L.S. to Lambert. Fish 266. ✛THE COPPERHEAD. By Fayette Hall. 1902. Fish 373. ✛HISTORICAL SOCIETY OF PENNSYLVANIA. (1865). Fish 742. ✛MAJOR GEN. GEORGE H. THOMAS. [By J. W. De Peyster] [New York, 1875] 2 A.L.S. to Lambert. ✛REMARKS of Lyman Trumbull . . . On the Seizure of Arsenals at Harpers Ferry, etc. [Washington, 1859] Autograph. Together five volumes, 8vo, half calf and three-quarter morocco.

80. CIVIL WAR. Collection of eight scarce pamphlets dealing with Civil War. 8vo, wrappers. 1861-65. War Powers of President, Causes of the War, etc.

81. CIVIL WAR HISTORY. A Collection of eleven volumes by DeGasparin (P.C.), E. A. Pollard, T. M. Eddy, J. A. Logan (A.L.S.), E. O. Haven (A.P.C.), C. E. Cheney, J. W. Brown, H. Haupt (Limited, signed) ; and "Trip of the Steamer Oceanus," (Fish 916) ; and American Annual Encyclopaedia, 1861. 1861-1901. Ten not in Fish or Oakleaf.

82. CLARK, DANIEL. EULOGY ON THE LIFE AND CHARACTER OF ABRAHAM LINCOLN. Manchester, N. H., 1865. 8vo, three-quarter morocco. 1000 copies. A.P.C. to Hart. Hart, Lambert copy. Fish 203.

83. CLAY AND LINCOLN. THE VIEWS AND SENTIMENTS OF HENRY CLAY AND ABRAHAM LINCOLN on the Slavery Question. No place [1860]. 8vo, 2 leaves. Very rare. Not in Fish or Oakleaf.

84. COGGESHALL, WILLIAM T. Lincoln Memorial. THE JOURNEYS OF ABRAHAM LINCOLN: From Springfield to Washington, 1861, and From Washington to Springfield, 1865. Columbus, 1865. 12mo, original cloth.
First edition. Rare. Superb copy. Fish 210.

85. [COLEMAN, WILLIAM MACON] THE EVIDENCE THAT ABRAHAM LINCOLN WAS NOT BORN IN LAWFUL WEDLOCK, or, The Sad Story of Nancy Hanks. [Dallas, Texas (?), 1899 (?)] 8vo, 8 leaves. Proof corrections in ink. Oakleaf 376.

86. COLFAX, SCHUYLER. LIFE AND PRINCIPLES OF ABRAHAM LINCOLN. Philadelphia, 1865. Two copies, 8vo, three-quarter morocco. 1000 copies. A.L.S. Burton collection. Fish 214.

87. COLLIS, CHARLES H. T. THE RELIGION OF ABRAHAM LINCOLN, Correspondence between C. H. T. Collis and R. G. Ingersoll. New York (1900). 12mo. A.P.C. ✣RELIGIOUS VIEWS OF ABRAHAM LINCOLN. Compiled by Orrin Henry Pennell. Alliance, Ohio [1904]. 8vo. Together two pamphlets, half calf. Fish 215 and 741.

88. CONFEDERATE PORTRAIT ALBUM. CONFEDERATE PORTRAIT ALBUM. Civil War, 1861-1865. No place, no date. 4to, decorated buckram.
Contains photographs of Jefferson Davis, A. H. Stephens, Generals and other officers. Laid in are 2 original photographs of the execution of the conspirators re assassination of Lincoln.

89. CONKLING, HENRY. AN INSIDE VIEW OF THE REBELLION and American Citizens' Text-Book. Chicago, 1864. 8vo, title wrappers, 12 leaves. Scarce 1864 campaign document, not in Fish or Oakleaf.

90. **[CONWAY, MONCURE D.]** The Rejected Stone; or, Insurrection vs. Resurrection in America. By a Native of Virginia. Boston, 1862. 12mo, original cloth. *Second edition. Rare. A.N.S. by Conway tipped in. A.P.C. from Publishers. Not in Fish or Oakleaf.*

91. **COOPER, JAMES.** The Death of President Lincoln. Philadelphia, 1865. 8vo, three-quarter morocco. 500 copies. A.P.C. Burton collection. Fish 224.

92. **COPPERHEAD.** A Collection of six pamphlets bound. The Copperhead Catechism. N. Y., 1864. The New Gospel of Peace. First, Second and Third Books. Tousey, N. Y., no date. A Few Words to the Thinking and Judicious Voters of Pennsylvania. No imprint. The Nasby Papers. Petroleum V. Nasby. Indianapolis, 1864. Fine collection in 12mo, three-quarter calf. Scarce pamphlets.

93. **COPPERHEAD CONVENTION.** Chicago Copperhead Convention. Washington, 1864. Unopened. Fish 190. ✛A Traitor's Peace. By a Democratic Workingman. Broadside, folio. ✛Lincoln or McClellan. Fish 512. ✛Col. Greene's Speech. Boston. Not in Fish or Oakleaf. ✛Campaign Document, No. 1. The Democratic Platform. Together five pamphlets, 8vo, wrappers, unbound.

94. **CORWIN, E.** Typed Manuscript. "Address." Honolulu, May 9, 1865. 4to, 4 pages. In folio, three-quarter morocco, boards. *Unpublished Address "delivered on the reception of the news of the murder of President Lincoln in Fort St. Church, Honolulu." Burton collection.*

95. **CRANE, C.** B. Sermon on the Occasion of the Death of President Lincoln. Hartford, 1865. 8vo, three-quarter morocco. 500 copies. A.L.S. to Hart re book. Hart, Lambert copy. Fish 231.

96. **CROCKER, SAMUEL** L. Eulogy upon the Character and Services of Abraham Lincoln. Boston, 1865. Two copies, 8vo, half calf and wrappers. 550 copies. A.P.C. Bound in are two poems by Bloodgood H. Cutter. Fish 233.

97. **CROOK, WILLIAM** H. Lincoln as I Knew Him. By William H. Crook (His Body-Guard). Compiled by Margarita S. Gerry. [Excerpts from Harper's Magazine, 1906-7] Large 8vo, three-quarter morocco. A.L.S. by Crook to Lambert. Lambert copy.

MRS. LINCOLN'S COPY

98. **CROSBY, FRANK.** Life of Abraham Lincoln. Philadelphia, 1865. 8vo, morocco, beveled covers, gilt edges, front cover stamped: "To Mrs. Lincoln, the Honored Wife of our late Honored and Lamented

President, with the Warmest Sympathies of the Publisher." Enclosed in half morocco, cloth slip case, inner wrapper.

First edition. Mrs. Lincoln's own copy. A.L.S., 8vo, one page, laid in. Written on mourning stationery, Chicago, April 9th, 1866. "I cannot recall whether I have replied to your note requesting the autograph of my deeply lamented husband, the President. . . ." Fish 234.

99. CUNNINGHAM, J. O. RECOLLECTIONS OF LINCOLN. [Reprinted from the Bibliotheca Sacra, October, 1908] 8vo, three-quarter straight grained calf. Burton collection. Oakleaf 407.

100. CURTIS, B. R. EXECUTIVE POWER. Cambridge, Printed by H. O. Houghton, 1862. 12mo. Variant issue of Fish 239. ✚THE COMMANDER-IN-CHIEF . . . An Answer to ex-judge Curtis' pamphlet. By Grosvenor P. Lowrey. New York, 1862. 12mo. A.P.C. Fish 606. ✚A LETTER TO THE HON. BENJAMIN R. CURTIS. By Charles P. Kirkland. New York, 1862. 8vo. A.P.C. Fish 488. ✚A LETTER TO PETER COOPER . . . Containing a Reprint of a Review of Judge Curtis' Paper . . . with a Letter from President Lincoln. By Charles P. Kirkland. New York, 1865. 8vo. A.L.S. re book. Fish 489. Together four pamphlets, original wrappers, in half morocco slip case, inner folder. Fine controversial collection.

101. (CURTIS, B. R.) THE POWER OF THE COMMANDER-IN-CHIEF to Declare Martial Law and Decree Emancipation: as Shown from B. R. Curtis. By Libertas [C. M. Ellis]. Boston, 1862. Large 8vo, cloth. A.P.C. by Ellis. McAleenan copy. Fish 510.

102. DAGGETT, O. E. A SERMON ON THE DEATH OF ABRAHAM LINCOLN. Canandaigua, N. Y., 1865. 12mo, three-quarter morocco. 750 copies. A.L.S. to Hart re book and MS. title page. Hart, Lambert, McAleenan copy. Fish 243.

103. DARLING, HENRY. GRIEF AND DUTY. Albany, 1865. 8vo, three-quarter morocco. 2000 copies. A.L.S. to Hart re book. Lambert copy. Fish 248.

104. DAVIDSON, JOHN. ADDRESS ON THE DEATH OF ABRAHAM LINCOLN. New York, 1865. 8vo, three-quarter morocco. A.P.C. Burton collection. Fish 250.

105. DAVIS, JEFFERSON. RELATIONS OF STATES. Baltimore, 1860. 8 leaves. ✚SPEECH . . . ON THE CONDITION OF THINGS IN SOUTH CAROLINA. Baltimore, 1861. 10 leaves, unopened. Together two pamphlets, 8vo, stitched.

106. DAVIS, J. McCAN. McClure's Magazine. ABRAHAM LINCOLN. [With] Ida M. Tarbell. New York, 1895-6. 8vo, morocco, gilt lettered cover; rubbed.

First appearance. Bound volume of excerpts from McClure's Magazine. A.L.S. by H. E. Barker laid in, testifying that this was Davis' own copy. "Story is particularly interesting in this form on acct of the profuse illustration, mostly omitted from later editions of the work." Serial publication of Fish 932.

107. DAVIS, J. McCAN. How Abraham Lincoln Became President. Springfield, 1908. Two copies, 16mo, original wrappers and rebound in cloth. ✚Same. Centennial Edition. 1909. 12mo, cloth. Together three volumes.
First and second editions. A.P.C. of each. Oakleaf 420, 421.

108. DAY, P. B. Memorial Discourse on the Character of Abraham Lincoln. Delivered at Hollis, N. H. Concord, 1865. 8vo, three-quarter morocco.
450 copies printed. A.L.S. to Hart re book. Contains the appreciative memoir of Lincoln published in the "London Star," which is seldom found elsewhere. Hart, Lambert copy. Fish 253.

109. DEAN, SIDNEY. Eulogy Pronounced in the City Hall, Providence, April 19. Providence, 1865. 8vo, three-quarter morocco. 1000 copies. A.P.C. Fish 255.

110. DEAN, SIDNEY. Eulogy . . . on the Occasion of the Funeral Solemnities of Abraham Lincoln. Providence, 1865. 8vo, three-quarter morocco. A.P.C. Burton collection. Fish 255.

111. DEBATE. The Great Debate. Souvenir. [*Frontispiece*] *A platform scene in the seven joint discussions between Lincoln and Douglas . . . Dome of State Capitol at Springfield.* [No imprint] Square 8vo, wrappers. Not in Fish or Oakleaf.

112. DEMING, HENRY C. Eulogy of Abraham Lincoln. Hartford, 1865. 3500 copies. A.P.C. to Hart. Fish 257. ✚HOLLAND, J. G. Eulogy on Abraham Lincoln. Springfield, 1865. 5000 copies. A.P.C. Fish 425. Together two volumes, 8vo, three-quarter morocco. Lambert copies.

113. DEPEW, CHAUNCEY M. Address. Galesburg, Ill., 1867. ✚BURTON, JOHN E. Abraham Lincoln. No place, 1903. Bound together in 8vo, three-quarter morocco, boards. Burton collection. Fish 261, (P.C.), 161.

114. DeWITT, DAVID MILLER. The Judicial Murder of Mary E. Surratt. Baltimore, 1895. Small 12mo, original cloth. First edition. Very scarce. Fish 264.

115. DODGE, DANIEL KILHAM. Abraham Lincoln: The Evolution of His Literary Style. Champaign, University Press, 1900. 4to, three-quarter morocco. T.L.S to Lambert re book. Lambert copy. Fish 275.

116. (DOUGLAS, STEPHEN A.) A Voter's Version of the Life and Character of Stephen Arnold Douglas. By Robert B. Warden. Columbus, 1860. A little foxed. ✚Life of Stephen A.

DOUGLAS, with His Most Important Speeches and Reports. By a Member of the Western Bar. New York, 1860. Together two volumes, 12mo, original cloth.

First editions. Oakleaf 1452. Second mentioned not in Fish or Oakleaf.

117. (DOUGLAS, STEPHEN A.) BOOK OF THE PROPHET STEPHEN, Son of Douglas. New York, Fecks & Bancker (1863). ✛SAME. Book Second. New York, J. F. Feeks (1864). Together two pamphlets, 16mo, glazed orange wrappers (two corners repaired) in half morocco, cloth slip case, inner folder. First editions. Fish 112, 113.

118. (DOUGLAS, STEPHEN A.) SAME. Green cover on Book Second. Edges of first mentioned rubbed. Fish 112, 113.

119. DRAPER, ANDREW S. THE ILLINOIS LIFE AND THE PRESIDENCY OF ABRAHAM LINCOLN. An Address at the University of Illinois, Lincoln's Birthday, 1896. 18mo. Fish 280. ✛LINCOLN. Albany, 1909. 8vo. T.L.S. Oakleaf 458. ✛ADDRESSES AND PAPERS, 1908-1909. Albany [1909]. 8vo. Two T.L.S. to Lambert. Not in Oakleaf. Together three volumes, three-quarter morocco. Lambert copies.

120. DRUMM, JOHN H. ASSASSINATION OF ABRAHAM LINCOLN. Bristol [Pa.], [1865]. 12mo, three-quarter morocco. 250 copies. A.P.C. to Hart. Hart, Lambert copy. Fish 281.

121. DUANE, RICHARD B. A SERMON . . . on the Day Appointed for the Funeral Obsequies of President Lincoln. Providence, 1865. 8vo, three-quarter morocco. 500 copies. A.D.S. re book. Lambert copy. Fish 283.

122. DUDLEY, JOHN L. DISCOURSE . . . on the Sabbath Morning after the Assassination of President Lincoln. Middletown [Conn.], 1865. 8vo, three-quarter morocco. 800 copies. A.L.S. to Hart re book. Hart, Lambert copy. Fish 284.

123. EARLY BIOGRAPHY. LIVES AND SPEECHES OF ABRAHAM LINCOLN [By W. D. Howells] AND HANNIBAL HAMLIN [By J. L. Hayes]. Columbus, O., 1860. ✛SAME. New York, 1860. ✛LIFE OF ABRAHAM LINCOLN . . . AND HANNIBAL HAMLIN. By J. H. Barrett. Cincinnati, 1860. ✛THE LIFE AND PUBLIC SERVICES OF HON. ABRAHAM LINCOLN AND HANNIBAL HAMLIN. By D. W. Bartlett. New-York, 1860. Together four volumes, 12mo, cloth.

First edition, first and second issues of first two. A.L.S. and T.L.S. by Howells in first two. Fish 597. First issue of last. Fish 75.

124. EDDY, RICHARD. "THE MARTYR TO LIBERTY." Three Sermons Preached in the First Universalist Church. Philadelphia, H. G. Leisenring's Steam-Power Printing House, 1865. Two copies, 8vo, three-quarter morocco and wrappers. First editions. 300 copies. A.P.C. Lambert copy. Fish 297.

125. EDGAR, CORNELIUS H. Josiah and Lincoln, the Great Reformers. Easton, Pa., 1865. 8vo, three-quarter morocco. 300 copies. Two A.L.S. to Hart re book. Hart, Lambert copy. Fish 300.

126. EDWARDS, HENRY L. Discourse Commemorative of Our Illustrious Martyr. Boston, 1865. Two copies, 8vo, three-quarter morocco and half calf. 500 copies. A.L.S. to Hart re book. A.L.S. to Boyd. Hart, Lambert copy, and Boyd copy. Fish 303.

127. EMERSON, RALPH. Mr. and Mrs. Ralph Emerson's Personal Recollections of Abraham Lincoln. Rockford, Ill., 1909. 8vo, three-quarter morocco. Burton collection. Oakleaf 483.

128. ESSAYS AND ADDRESSES. Speeches and Addresses of the late Hon. David Coddington. New York, 1866. ✠Official Documents, Addresses, etc. of George Opdyke, Mayor, During 1862 and 1863. New York, 1866. ✠Tribune Essays. By Charles T. Congdon. New York, 1869. ✠"Warrington" Pen-Portraits. Edited by Mrs. W. S. Robinson. Boston, 1877. Together four volumes, 8vo, cloth.
First editions. A.L.S. by Opdyke and Congdon laid in. A.P.C. of first two.

129. EVERETT, C. C. A Sermon. Bangor, 1865. 8vo, wrappers. 600 copies. A.P.C. and A.L.S. Fish 312.

130. EVERETT, EDWARD. An Oration Delivered on the Battle-field of Gettysburg, at the Consecration of the Cemetery. [With] Interesting Reports of the Dedicatory Ceremonies, etc. New York, 1863. 8vo, original printed wrappers.
First edition. A.L.S. by Everett. Fish says: "Contains Lincoln's [Gettysburg address] probably its first appearance in book form; also reports of the occasion by correspondents of the Tribune, Herald, World and Times of New York." Fish 314.

131. EXECUTIVE POWER. The Executive Power of the United States. Translated from Adolphe de Chambrun by Mrs. Dahlgren. Lancaster, Pa., 1874. 12mo. ✠War Powers under the Constitution of the United States. By Wm. Whiting. Boston, 1871. 8vo. Together two volumes, cloth.
First edition of first. A.P.C. to Geo. Bancroft with Lenox Library book plate. A.P.C. of second to Seth Ames, Judge of the Supreme Court.

132. FARQUHAR, JOHN. The Claims of God to Recognition in the Assassination of President Lincoln. Lancaster, Pa., 1865. 8vo, half calf. 1000 copies. A. Envelope Address to Hart. MS. corrections in text. Hart, Lambert copy. Fish 319.

133. FISH, DANIEL. Lincoln Bibliography, A List of Books and Pamphlets Relating to Abraham Lincoln. New York (1906). Large 8vo, original cloth, gilt top; slightly shaken.
Limited to 75 copies, signed by Fish, of which only 40 were for sale. This is labeled No. 5, the compiler's copy, and belonged to William H. Lambert, whose

signature appears on the fly leaf and whose magnificent collection of Lincoln material was sold in 1914. Oakleaf 501.

134. FISH, DANIEL. LINCOLN COLLECTIONS AND LINCOLN BIBLIOGRAPHY. New York, Printed for the Bibliographical Society of America, 1909. 8vo, wrappers.

135. FISH, DANIEL. LEGAL PHASES OF THE LINCOLN AND DOUGLAS DEBATES. Annual Address before the State Bar Association of Minnesota. Reprinted from the Proceedings, 1909. 8vo, three-quarter morocco. A.L.S. to Maj. Lambert, 1908. Lambert copy. Oakleaf 502.

136. FISH, DANIEL. A REPRINT OF THE LIST OF BOOKS AND PAMPHLETS RELATING TO ABRAHAM LINCOLN. Rock Island, Ill., 1926. Large 8vo, three-quarter morocco cloth, gilt top. Limited to 102 copies, signed by Oakleaf.

137. FOWLER, C. H. AN ORATION on the Character and Public Services of Abraham Lincoln. Chicago, 1867. 8vo, three-quarter morocco. Burton collection. Scarce. Fish 327.

138. FOWLER, H. ALFRED. CHARACTER AND DEATH OF ABRAHAM LINCOLN. Auburn, N. Y., 1865. 8vo, three-quarter morocco. 500 copies. Two A.L.S. to Hart re book. Hart, Lambert copy. Fish 328.

139. FOWLER, H. ALFRED. LINCOLNIANA BOOK PLATES AND COLLECTIONS. [*Portrait*] Kansas City, 1913. Square 16mo, half cloth, boards, boxed. A.P.C. from Oakleaf. Signed by Fowler. Engraved book plates of Oakleaf, Stewart and Fowler. Oakleaf 510.

140. FOWLER, JOHN. AN ADDRESS ON THE DEATH OF PRESIDENT LINCOLN. At New Rochelle, N. Y. New-York, 1865. Large 8vo, three-quarter morocco. 930 copies, untrimmed. A.L.S. to Hart re book. Autograph of H. B. Dawson, the historian, on wrapper. Hart, Lambert copy. Fish 329.

141. GAY, W. H. TYPED MANUSCRIPT SIGNED. "Lincoln and Quincy in the Civil War." 4to, 8 pages.
Autograph inscription on separate leaf: "This address I delivered before the Quincy Historical Society on the 14th day of April 1913. W. H. Gay. Late Capt. of the First Iowa Battery." Laid in are 2 T.L.S. by T. E. Musselman of Quincy relating to the address which had been wrongly attributed to Geo. E. Adams; and newspaper clipping of article by W. C. Scott. Not in Oakleaf.

WITH A.L.S. BY LAMBERT LAID IN, CONSIDERING AND COLLATING THE HAY MS. WITH THE BALTIMORE DRAFT

142. GETTYSBURG ADDRESS. PRESIDENT LINCOLN'S ADDRESS AT GETTYSBURG. *Photographed from the Original Manuscript.* No place, 1905. Folio, cloth.
Limited to 6 copies. Laid in is A.L.S. by William H. Lambert, 4to; 4 pages; Philadelphia April 19, 1909; to John P. Nicholson. Important critical letter, in

which Lambert states his reasons for considering the Baltimore MS. the final draft and gives a full collation of the differences in the two MSS. Not in Fish or Oakleaf.

143. GILLETTE, A. D. GOD SEEN ABOVE ALL NATIONAL CALAMITIES. Washington, D. C., 1865. 8vo, half calf. 2500 copies. A.P.C. Lambert copy. Fish 346.

144. GORE, J. ROGERS. TYPED MANUSCRIPT. "The Boyhood of Abraham Lincoln." 4to, 162 pages. ✚THE BOYHOOD OF ABRAHAM LINCOLN, From the Spoken Narratives of Austin Gollaher. *Illustrated from photographs.* Indianapolis (1921). 12mo, original cloth, jacket. Together two pieces.

The original MS. with autograph corrections and directions to the printer together with the first edition of the published book, autographed on fly leaf. Oakleaf 564.

145. GROLIER CLUB. CATALOGUE OF A COLLECTION OF ENGRAVED AND OTHER PORTRAITS OF LINCOLN. New York, 1899. 16mo, three-quarter morocco. Introduction by C. H. Hart. Fish 365.

146. Withdrawn.

147. HALL, FAYETTE. THE SECRET AND POLITICAL HISTORY OF THE WAR OF THE REBELLION. In twelve numbers. No. 1. [Only one printed] New Haven, Conn., 1890. Large 8vo, half calf. Author's copy, signed. Prospectus for work with MS. corrections bound in. Fish 373, Oakleaf 594. Disparages Lincoln.

148. HALL, GORDON. PRESIDENT LINCOLN'S DEATH; Its Voice to the People. A Discourse. Northampton, Mass., 1865. 8vo, three-quarter morocco. A.L.S. to Hart re book. Hart, Lambert copy. Fish 374.

PRESENTED TO LAMBERT BY STEWART

149. HAMPTON ROADS CONFERENCE, THE. LINCOLN'S ACCOUNT OF THE HAMPTON ROADS CONFERENCE. *With facsimiles from the original documents in the collection of Judd Stewart.* Privately printed, 1910. Folio, half grey cloth, boards; slightly soiled.

A.P.C. inscribed from one great collector on Lincoln material to another: "Maj. Wm. H. Lambert With kindest regards Judd Stewart." Oakleaf 599.

150. HART, CHARLES HENRY. A BIOGRAPHICAL SKETCH OF HIS EXCELLENCY ABRAHAM LINCOLN, Late President of the United States. Large 8vo, half cloth, boards.

Limited to 100 copies, printed for private circulation. A.P.C. from Hart to Mrs. Moore, Trenton Falls, with full-page inscription quoting praise from W. C. Bryant, W. H. Herndon, R. H. Dana Jr. and C. F. Adams. Burton collection. Fish 394.

151. HAVEN, GILBERT. THE UNITER AND LIBERATOR OF AMERICA. Boston, 1865. 8vo, three-quarter morocco. 500 copies. A.L.S. to Hart re book. Hart, Lambert copy. Fish 398.

152. HAY, JOHN. THE REPUBLICAN PARTY. By John Hay and Elihu Root. New York, Privately printed, 1904. Two copies, 4to, original printed wrappers.

153. HERNDON, WILLIAM H. HERNDON'S LINCOLN, The True Story of a Great Life. The History and Personal Recollections of Abraham Lincoln by William H. Herndon, For Twenty Years His Friend and Law Partner and Jesse William Weik. [*Illustrated*] Three volumes. Chicago, Belford-Clarke Co., 1890. 12mo, original cloth, gilt tops.

First edition. First issue: with correct imprint. Rare suppressed edition. Magnificent set of the greatest and most intimate biography of Lincoln. Fish 409.

154. HERNDON, WILLIAM H. ABRAHAM LINCOLN, Miss Ann Rutledge, New Salem, Pioneering, The Poem. Springfield, Ill., 1910. Narrow 4to, buckram, morocco label, unopened.

Limited to 150 copies, signed by H. E. Barker. Eight sheets of the original prospectus laid in. Also A.L.S. and T.L.S. by Barker. Oakleaf 618.

155. HERNDON, WILLIAM H. LINCOLN'S RELIGION. Original large sheet cut in strips and pasted into 8vo, cloth album.

Very rare. A.L.S. by Barker to Maj. Lambert: "This lecture was published in one large sheet—blank on back, and on account of the perishable shape very few have been preserved. Even our State Library hasn't a copy, and in fact this is the first one I have found in all my search after such things. I bought this from one of our old citizens who heard the lecture before a 'crowd' of less than three dozen. He had cut it up . . ." Many clippings and photographs pasted in. Not in Fish or Oakleaf.

156. HERTZ, EMANUEL. A collection of thirteen pamphlets on Lincoln, 1930, 1931. 8vo, wrappers.

Includes; The Grand Street Boys; His Law Partners, Clerks and Boys; Lincoln of Illinois; Lincoln's Diplomacy; The Wizardry of Lincoln's Political Appointments; Lincoln in Excelsis; Face to Face with; The Religion of; "Pew 89," Lincoln and Beecher; His Favorite Poems and Poets; Children's Lincoln; Lincoln's Spells of Gloom; and His Inventive Mind.

157. HIBBARD, A. G. IN MEMORY OF ABRAHAM LINCOLN. Detroit, 1865. 8vo, half calf. 200 copies. (Fish corrected.) A.L.S. by E. E. Lamb to Hart re sermon. Hart, Lambert copy. Fish 412.

158. HILL, FREDERICK TREVOR. ABRAHAM LINCOLN. The Battle of the Giants. [With] The Parents of Lincoln. By Ida M. Tarbell. An Appeal to Patriotism. By Richard Lloyd Jones. The Lincoln Farm Association, 1907. 16mo, half cloth, boards. ✛LINCOLN'S LEGACY OF INSPIRATION. New York (1909). Tall 16mo, half cloth, boards. ✛LINCOLN THE LAWYER. New York, 1913. 8vo, three-quarter morocco, boards, gilt top. Together three volumes.

First editions of first two mentioned. Second is A.P.C. to Maj. Lambert. Oakleaf 160 and 652. Limited to 800 copies of third mentioned, with menu and book plate. Later edition of Oakleaf 651.

159. HISTORICAL FICTION. THE GRAYSONS. By Edward Eggleston. New York, (1887). ✛ON THE WING OF OCCASIONS. By Joel Chandler Harris. New York, 1900. ✛THE PRARIE SCHOONER.

By William E. Barton. Boston, (1900). ✛THE CRISIS. By Winston Churchill. New York, 1901. Together four volumes, 8vo, original cloth.

First editions. First binding of second mentioned and first issue of fourth mentioned: with "its" page 257, 2nd line from the bottom. A.L.S. by Eggleston, 12mo, 3 pages.

160. **HOBSON, J. T.** THE LINCOLN YEAR BOOK, Containing Immortal Words of Abraham Lincoln. Dayton, Ohio, 1912. 12mo, three-quarter morocco, boards, gilt top.

First edition. Book plate, A.L.S., menu and pamphlet of Association. Autographed by H. C. Lodge, F. B. Willis, W. Jayne, E. B. Rogers, J. W. Bunn, etc. Facsimile of the election of Lincoln as a trustee laid in. Oakleaf 683.

161. **HOLDOM, JESSE.** LINCOLN CENTENNIAL ADDRESS, at McKinley High School, Chicago. February 12, 1909. Bound with: LINCOLN CENTENNIAL ADDRESS, before the West End Woman's Club, Chicago. 1909. 8vo, three-quarter morocco. P.C. with T.L.S. to Lambert. Oakleaf 687 and 688.

162. **HOUSER, M. L.** THE BOOKS THAT LINCOLN READ. Peoria, Ill., 1929. 8vo, wrappers in original envelope. Limited to 100 copies.

SECOND KNOWN BIOGRAPHY

163. **HOWARD, J. Q.** THE LIFE OF ABRAHAM LINCOLN: with Extracts from his Speeches. Columbus, Follett, Foster and Company, 1860. 12mo, full calf.

Rare. The second known biography of Lincoln. Fish says: "A Prefatory note is dated June 26, 1860, on which day the work was printed. Next to the 'Wigwam Edition' (Fish 1052), the above is apparently the pioneer biography, the Scripps Life not being copyrighted until July." Autograph note on fly leaf signed by J. E. B[urton].: "This book was really unknown to Boyd or Fish or any Lincoln collector until Oct. 21—1901 when 22 copies were found in New York—The First sold at auction for $25.00 and will no doubt command much higher figures." Fish 431.

164. **HUBBARD, ELBERT.** LITTLE JOURNEYS TO THE HOMES OF AMERICAN STATESMEN. Abraham Lincoln. New York (1898). 16mo, three-quarter morocco. First edition. T.L.S. to J. S. Little. Fish 434.

165. **HUMOUR.** THE ORPHEUS C. KERR PAPERS. [By R. C. Newall] New York, 1862. ✛CHRONICLES OF THE GREAT REBELLION. By Allen M. Scott. Cincinnati, 1863. ✛WAR LETTERS OF A DISBANDED VOLUNTEER. [By Joseph Barber] New York, 1864. Fish 1017. ✛THE LIFE AND ADVENTURES OF PRIVATE MILES O'REILLY. [C. G. Halpine] *With comic illustrations by Mullen.* New York, 1864. ✛BAKED MEATS OF THE FUNERAL. By Private Miles O'Reilly. New York, 1866. ✛LETTERS OF MAJOR JACK DOWNING. [C. A. Davis] New York, 1866. ✛ARTEMUS WARD, His Book. New York, 1865. Together seven volumes, 12mo, original cloth.

First editions of first five mentioned. Good collection of Civil war humour, several of them Lincoln's favorites.

166· HYLTON, J. DUNBAR. The Praesidicide: A Poem. Philadelphia, 1868. 18mo, original bright blue cloth.

First edition. First issue: with 194 pages. Very rare first issue of Fish 441, of which only a few copies are known. A.P.C., in pencil. The poem is laid in Maryland to which Booth made his escape, and gives the most striking events in the history of the conspiracy.

167. ILES, MAJ. ELIJAH. Sketches of Early Life and Times in Kentucky, Missouri and Illinois. Springfield, 1883. 8vo, original cloth.

First edition. Scarce and early reminiscences of a Major in the Black Hawk War. Portrait inserted. Fine copy.

168. ILLINOIS. Death of Lincoln. Proceedings in the Supreme Court of Illinois. Chicago, 1865. 8vo, glazed black wrappers; rubbed at edges.

169. ILLINOIS. Abraham Lincoln. Proceedings in the Supreme Court of Illinois Commemorating the 100th Anniversary of his Birth. [No place, 1909] 8vo, three-quarter morocco. Scarce. A.P.C. by Oakleaf to Lambert. Not in Oakleaf.

170. ILLINOIS CENTRAL RAILROAD COMPANY. Abraham Lincoln as Attorney for the Illinois Central Railroad Company. [*Illustrated*] No place, 1905. Folio, full limp seal.
Limited to 200 copies of the third edition. Fish 7.

171. ILLINOIS-MICHIGAN CANAL. Report of a Majority of the Board of Trustees of the Illinois and Michigan Canal, Made in Reply to Certain Charges . . . by Mr. Charles Oakley, etc. Washington, 1847. 8vo, wrappers. 34 leaves. Rare. Not in Buck.

172. INAUGURALS. Abraham Lincoln. First and Second Inaugural Addresses, Message, July 5, 1861, Proclamation, January 1, 1863, Gettysburg Address, November 19, 1863. Washington, 1909. 4to, three-quarter morocco. Only a few copies for exclusive use of senators. Two T.L.S. re scarcity of book. Lambert copy. Oakleaf 715.

173. INGERSOLL, ROBERT G. Abraham Lincoln. New York, 1907. 4to. +Same. 1907. 12mo. Together two volumes, three-quarter morocco.
Limited to 100 copies of first on Japan vellum. A. Check S. by Ingersoll. Oakleaf 726, and later issue of Fish 448.

174. IRISH, E. M. Abraham Lincoln. [Kalamazoo (?), 1907] 8vo, three-quarter morocco. A.P.C. from Judd Stewart to Lambert. Lambert copy. Oakleaf 730.

175. IVES, ALFRED E. Victory Turned into Mourning. Bangor, 1865. 8vo, three-quarter morocco. 250 copies. A.L.S. to Hart re book. Hart, Lambert copy. Fish 456.

176. **JOHNSON, HERRICK.** "God's Ways Unsearchable." A Discourse on the Death of President Lincoln . . . in Mozart Hall. Pittsburgh [1865]. 12mo, three-quarter morocco. Rare. A.P.C. Lambert copy. Fish 465. ◦

177. **JONES, JENKIN LLOYD.** Nancy Hanks Lincoln, A Sermon. Reprinted from Unity of February 12, 1903. Chicago [1903]. 12mo, three-quarter morocco. Autographed. Two T.L.S. to Little, saying the book is rare and that the author himself has no copy. Fish 471.

178. **JORDAN, E. S.** Death of Abraham Lincoln. A Discourse . . . at . . . Cumberland Centre, Me. Portland, 1865. 8vo, three-quarter morocco. 275 copies. A.L.S. re book. Lambert copy. Fish 474.

179. **JOSEPH, PHILIP.** The Fame of Abraham Lincoln. Moline, 1905. 4to, wrappers. 50 copies. A.P.C. to Little by Oakleaf. Fish 475.

180. **JUVENILE BIOGRAPHY.** The Children's Life of Abraham Lincoln. By M. Louise Putnam. Chicago, 1892. 12mo. ✝Abraham Lincoln. By Charles C. Coffin. New York, 1893. 8vo. ✝The True Story of Abraham Lincoln. By Elbridge S. Brooks. Boston (1896). 4to. ✝The Boy's Life of Lincoln. By Helen Nicolay. New York, 1906. 12mo. Together four volumes, original cloth.
First editions. All illustrated. Autograph 10 line inscription signed in second mentioned. Fish 781, 209, 138; Oakleaf 1038.

181. **KAMENSKAVO, A.** The Lives of Celebrated Men. Biographical Library. Abraham Lincoln, His Life and Public Achievements. *With a portrait of Lincoln engraved in Leipzig by Hedan.* St. Petersburg, 1891. (Transliterated from Russian characters.) 12mo, three-quarter straight grained calf. MS. translation of Preface. Lambert copy, Fish 480.

182. **KECKLEY, ELIZABETH.** Behind the Scenes: or, Thirty Years a Slave, and Four Years in the White House. New York, 1868. 12mo, original cloth.
First edition. Very scarce. Attempt made to suppress on publication. E. Keckley describes herself as "Formerly a slave, but more recently modiste, and friend to Mrs. Abraham Lincoln." The accounts of her dealings with Mrs. Lincoln do little to gild that lady's character. Fish says: "Incredible but for accompanying documents." Beautiful copy. Fish 481.

183. **KEELING, R. J.** The Death of Moses. Washington, 1865. 8vo, wrappers. 500 copies. A.L.S. re book, MS. corrections. Fish 482.

184. **[KIRKLAND, CHARLES P.]** The Coming Contraband; a Reason against the Emancipation Proclamation, not given by Mr. Justice Curtis, to whom it is addressed by an Officer in the Field. New-York,

G. P. Putnam, 1862. 16mo, wrappers; name crossed out on title. Autographed. Rare pamphlet. Not in Fish.

185. LAMB, E. E. Sermon on the Death of' President Lincoln. Preached in . . . Rootstown [Ohio], April 23, 1865. [No imprint] 8vo, stitched, 8 leaves. 200 copies. Fish 495.

186. LAMBERT, WILLIAM H. Memorial Day Oration, at the National Cemetery, Arlington, Va. Philadelphia, 1883. 8vo, three-quarter morocco. A.P.C. to Govnr. Pennypacker by Lambert. Not in Fish or Oakleaf.

VERY RARE PAMPHLET

187. LAMBERT, WILLIAM H. Abraham Lincoln . . . Annual Oration delivered before the Society of the Army of the Potomac. Pittsburgh, October 11, 1899. 4to, half calf: A.P.C. on wrapper erased.
Very rare pamphlet. 40 copies printed. In 1907 D. Newhall stated: "I have had only 2 and Lambert has only 2 left, not for disposal." Fish 496.

188. LAMBERT, WILLIAM H. A Lincoln Correspondence. Reprinted from the Century Magazine, 1909. Oakleaf 779. ✛In Memoriam, William Harrison Lambert. New York, the Lincoln Fellowship, 1912. 250 copies. A.L.S., 2pp. by Lambert re books wanted. Together two pamphlets, 8vo, original wrappers.

189. LAMBERT, WILLIAM H. Abraham Lincoln 1809-1909. Lincoln Literature. [Philadelphia (?), 1909] Square 8vo, three-quarter morocco. Lambert's own copy. Oakleaf 780.

190. LAMBERT, WILLIAM H. Versions of the Gettysburg Address, Cited in "The Gettysburg Address—When Written, How Received, Its True Form." No place [1909]. Square 12mo, three-quarter morocco. With page vii cancelled and leaf inserted. Oakleaf 781.

190-A. LAMBERT, WILLIAM H. Abraham Lincoln, Address delivered before the Union League of Philadelphia. February 12, 1909. 8vo, three-quarter calf. A.P.C. to John E. Burton. Fish 782.

191. LAMON, WARD HILL. The Life of Abraham Lincoln: from His Birth to his Inauguration as President. *With illustrations.* Boston, 1872. Thick 8vo, original cloth, beveled edges.
First edition. Very scarce. Beautiful copy. Book plates of John S. Little and Thomas MacKellar. Fish 498.

192. LAMON, WARD HILL. Recollections of Abraham Lincoln 1847-1865. Edited by Dorothy Lamon Teillard. [*Illustrated*] Washington, 1911. 12mo, original cloth.
Second edition, revised. Autographed by Mrs. Teillard. Superb copy. Oakleaf 790.

193. LATHROP, GEORGE PARSONS. Gettysburg: A Battle Ode. Read before the Army of the Potomac, at Gettysburg, July 3, 1888. New York, 1888. 12mo, three-quarter morocco. First edition. A.P.C. and A.L.S. re book. Not in Fish or Oakleaf.

194. LEE, JAMES W. Services in Commemoration of the One Hundredth Anniversary of the Birth of Abraham Lincoln. Arranged by Union and Confederate Veterans. Atlanta, Georgia, 1909. 8vo, three-quarter morocco. Two A.L.S. re book to Lambert. Oakleaf 805.

195. LELAND, CHARLES GODFREY. Abraham Lincoln and the Abolition of Slavery in the United States. New York, 1879. 12mo, original cloth. ✛ Same. Three-quarter morocco, boards. Together two volumes.

First American editions. First and second issues: with 246 and 250 pages respectively and with publisher's note preceding the Preface of second mentioned, explaining that all errors have been corrected. 2 A.L.S. by Leland tipped in second issue, to Charles H. Hart and Mrs. Botta, dated 1866 and 1871. Very fine copies. Fish 504, note.

196. LETTERS AND SAYINGS. Abraham Lincoln's Pen and Voice. Edited by G. M. Van Buren. Cincinnati, 1890. ✛ Lincoln, Passages from His Speeches and Letters. Introduction by R. W. Gilder. New York, 1901. ✛ Lincolnics. Collected by H. Llewellyn Williams. New York (1906). ✛ The Lincoln Year Book. Compiled by Wallace Rice. Chicago, 1907. ✛ Letters and Addresses of Abraham Lincoln. New York, 1904. ✛ Oratory. Introduction by J. Bryce. London (1909). Together six volumes; first editions of first four. Fish 1004, 570; Oakleaf 1505, 1177.

197. LETTERS. Uncollected Letters of Abraham Lincoln. Now first brought together by Gilbert A. Tracy. With an Introduction by Ida M. Tarbell. Boston, 1917. Half buckram, boards, unopened. ✛ New Letters and Papers of Lincoln. Compiled by Paul M. Angle. *With illustrations.* Boston, 1930. Cloth. Together two volumes, 8vo, jackets.

Limited to 550 copies of first mentioned, autographed by Tracy. Oakleaf 1414. First edition of second mentioned. Fine copies.

198. LEVY, T. AARON. Lincoln, the Politician. Boston (1918). 12mo, cloth, jacket. First edition. A.P.C. Oakleaf 815.

GETTYSBURG EDITION DE GRAND LUXE

199. LINCOLN, ABRAHAM. Complete Works of Abraham Lincoln. Edited by John G. Nicolay and John Hay. Twelve volumes. New York, Francis D. Tandy Co., 1905. Three-quarter morocco, boards, gilt tops, jackets. ✛ Prospectus. *With frontispieces.* Limp morocco. Together thirteen volumes, 8vo.

Limited to 300 sets of the Grand Luxe Gettysburg Edition. The most complete edition of Lincoln's works, made under the scrupulous editing of Nicolay and Hay who were his private secretaries and personal friends particularly during the crowded presidential years. Fish 573.

200. LINCOLN, ABRAHAM. COMPLETE WORKS OF ABRAHAM LINCOLN. Edited by John G. Nicolay and John Hay. [*Illustrated*] Twelve volumes. New York, F. D. Tandy (1905). 8vo, cloth, gilt tops. The Biographical edition. Fine.

201. LINCOLN, ABRAHAM. THE WRITINGS OF ABRAHAM LINCOLN. Edited by Arthur Brooks Lapsley. With an Introduction by Theodore Roosevelt. Eight volumes. New York, 1905, 1906. Large 8vo, buckram, gilt tops, jackets.
Limited to 600 sets of the Collector's Federal edition. Fine set. ·Fish 574.

202. LINCOLN, ABRAHAM. DISCOVERIES AND INVENTIONS, A Lecture by Abraham Lincoln. Delivered in 1860. San Francisco, John Howell, 1915. 8vo, boards, unopened, slip case.
Limited to 250 copies on Fabriano paper, under the direction of John Henry Nash. Autographed by Henry A. Melvin, owner of the MS. from which the book was printed. Prospectuses laid in. Oakleaf 862.

203. LINCOLN, ABRAHAM. IN MEMORIAM. No place, no date. 8vo, three-quarter morocco.
Scarce. Contains Farewell Speech, Emancipation Proclamation, Gettysburg Address, Inaugural Address and Poem. Not in Fish or Oakleaf.

204. [LINCOLN, ABRAHAM] HALE'S HISTORY OF THE UNITED STATES, From their First Settlement as Colonies, etc. New York, 1835. 16mo, half morocco, original printed boards; worn.
Lincoln's school book, with signature "A. Lincoln 1837" in faded ink on the title page. This book was presented by Lincoln to his friend, Wm. H. Berrian, architect, who gave it to his daughter, Florence M., who passed it on to Bishop W. C. Doane. Mr. Little purchased the volume at the auction of the Doane library in 1914.

205. LINCOLN. TRIBUNE TRACTS.—No. 4. National Politics. Speech of Abraham Lincoln, of Illinois, Delivered at the Cooper Institute, Monday Feb. 27, 1860. 8vo, stitched. Very scarce. Fish 529.

206. LINCOLN. PRESIDENT LINCOLN'S VIEWS, An Important Letter on the Principle Involved in the Vallandigham Case. Philadelphia, 1863. 8vo, unbound. Fish 546.

207. LINCOLN. THE MARTYR'S MONUMENT. Being the Patriotism and Political Wisdom of Abraham Lincoln. New York (1865). Red cloth. ✚SAME. Black cloth. Together two volumes, 12mo, beveled edges.
First editions. Two varieties of binding. Nicolay's own copy of first mentioned, with inscription: "R. C. McCormick to Jno. G. Nicolay." McCormick's autograph on title page. Interesting association item. Fish 553.

208. LINCOLN. OLD SOUTH LEAFLETS. No. 1. Lincoln's Inaugurals, etc. 12mo. Lambert copy. Fish 541. ✚THE GETTYSBURG SPEECH and Other Papers. Riverside Literature Series. No. 32. Boston, 1871. 16mo. Book plate of Judd Stewart. Not in Fish. Together two volumes, three-quarter morocco.

209. LINCOLN ANECDOTA. Anecdotes of Abraham Lincoln. Edited by J. B. McClure. Chicago, 1879. 8vo. ✛Anecdotal Lincoln. Biographical Sketch by Paul Selby. *Fully illustrated.* Chicago, 1900. 8vo. ✛Story of Abraham Lincoln. By Eleanor Gridley. Chicago, 1927. Large 8vo. ✛Lincoln's Yarns and Stories. Edited by A. K. McClure. *Profusely illustrated.* Chicago, no date. 8vo. Together four volumes, original cloth.

First editions of first two mentioned. Fish 619 and Oakleaf 1258 and 582 respectively. A.L.S. by Selby. A.P.C., signed of third mentioned, with A.N.S. and T.L.S. by E. Gridley and prospectuses. Very fine copies.

210. LINCOLN AS HERO. Abraham Lincoln, the Type of American Genius. By Rufus Blanchard. Wheaton, 1882. Cloth. ✛The Martyrs and Heroes of Illinois. Edited by James Barnet. *Illustrated.* Chicago, 1865. Three-quarter morocco. ✛Politics and Politicians. By D. W. Lusk. Springfield, Ill., 1884. Calf. Together three volumes, 8vo. First editions. A.P.C. of first mentioned, scarce. Fish 105.

211. LINCOLN'S BIRTHPLACE. House of Representatives. 60th Congress. Report No. 1641. [Washington, 1908] 8vo, 2 leaves. To aid Lincoln Farm Assn. building a memorial at Lincoln's birthplace. Not in Oakleaf.

212. LINCOLN'S CABINET. Lincoln and His Cabinet. By C. A. Dana. Cleveland, 1896. 16mo, half cloth, boards. ✛The Life and Public Services of Salmon Portland Chase. By J. W. Shuckers. New York, 1874. 8vo, cloth. ✛An Address on the Life, Character and Services of William H. Seward. By C. F. Adams. Albany, 1873. Tall 8vo, cloth. ✛Lincoln and Seward. By Gideon Welles. New York, 1874. 12mo, cloth. ✛Greeley on Lincoln. Edited by Joel Benton. New York, (1893). 12mo, cloth. Together five volumes.

Limited to 350 copies of first. First editions of last four. A.L.S. and autographs by S. P. Chase, C. F. Adams, Gideon Welles, Horace Greeley and J. Benton. Fish 245, (Shuckers not in Fish), 20, 1031, 362.

213. LINCOLN CENTENNIAL ASSOCIATION. `Lincoln Centennial Association Papers. Six volumes. Springfield, 1924-1929. 8vo, half cloth, boards. Fine.

214. LINCOLN CENTENNIAL ASSOCIATION. Duplicates of above for 1924, 1927, 1928, 1929. Together four volumes. Fine.

215. LINCOLN-DOUGLAS DEBATES. Political Debates between Hon. Abraham Lincoln and Hon. Stephen Douglas, in the Celebrated Campaign of 1858, in Illinois. Columbus, Follett, Foster and Company, 1860. 8vo, original cloth. Illinois State Historical Society. The Lincoln-Douglas Debates. Edited by Edwin E. Sparks. Springfield, 1908. Thick 8vo, three-quarter morocco, boards, gilt top. Together two volumes.

First edition of first mentioned. A.L.S. by Douglas laid in. Dated: "U. S. Senate Jany. 19 1858." To: J. E. Chase, North Conway, N. H." Sending autograph. Fish 586. Second mentioned souvenir volume of the 102nd Anniversary of Lincoln's birth. A.P.C. to John E. Burton. Book plate. Oakleaf 62.

216. LINCOLN-DOUGLAS DEBATES. THE LINCOLN-DOUGLAS DEBATES, Fifty Years After. By F. T. Hill. [Excerpt from the Century Magazine, Nov. 1908] 4to. Two A.L.S. re book. ✛SEMI-CENTENNIAL OF THE LINCOLN-DOUGLAS DEBATES IN ILLINOIS. By F. G. Blair. Springfield, Ill., 1908. 8vo. A.P.C. by Oakleaf to Lambert. Together two volumes, three-quarter morocco. Lambert copies.

217. LINCOLN FELLOWSHIP. THE LINCOLN FELLOWSHIP. First Annual Meeting, 1908. 2 copies. ✛SAME. 1909-1910. ✛SAME. 1911. 4 copies, one in three-quarter morocco. Together seven volumes, 8vo, six wrappers. Oakleaf 494, 495, 496.

218. LINCOLN IN ILLINOIS. LINCOLN IN ILLINOIS. By Octavia Roberts. *Drawings by Lester G. Hornby.* Boston, 1918. Half cloth, boards, jacket. ✛TRANSACTIONS OF THE McCLEAN COUNTY HISTORICAL SOCIETY. Bloomington, 1900. Cloth. ✛FREEPORT'S LINCOLN. By W. T. Raleigh. Freeport, 1930. Cloth. Together three volumes, 8vo.

Limited to 1000 copies, signed of first. First editions of last two. Oakleaf 1188. Fish 628 ("A valuable contribution to history of the 'lost speech' convention."), (Raleigh later than Oakleaf.).

219. LINCOLN MEMORIAL. THE BIRTHPLACE OF ABRAHAM LINCOLN. Official Papers Establishing the Marriage of His Parents. Compiled by Lincoln Memorial Company, Louisville, Ky., no date. 3¼" x 5½", printed wrappers, mounted on leaf in 8vo, three-quarter morocco, boards, in half morocco, cloth slip case, inner cloth wrapper.

Rare pamphlet. Bound in are copies of the marriage bond of Thomas Lincoln and Nancy Hanks, parents of Abraham, and a list of the marriages by Jesse Head, Methodist Minister, who performed the ceremony. All signed and attested by W. F. Booker, Clerk of Washington County Court, Ky. Also a 3 page A.L.S. by W. F. Booker explaining the papers. Lambert collection. Oakleaf 173.

220. LINCOLN OBSEQUIES. THE LINCOLN MEMORIAL. Edited by John G. Shay. New York, 1865. 8vo. ✛THE NATION'S TRIBUTE TO ABRAHAM LINCOLN. Compiled by B. F. Morris. Washington, 1865. 8vo. ✛SERMONS Preached in Boston on the Death of Abraham Lincoln. Boston, 1865. 12mo. ✛OBSEQUIES OF ABRAHAM LINCOLN IN UNION SQUARE. New York, 1865. 8vo. ✛OBSEQUIES OF ABRAHAM LINCOLN, in the City of New York. 1866. 4to. Together five volumes, cloth.

First editions. A.P.C. of fourth mentioned to E. M. Stanton. Not in Fish or Oakleaf.

221. LINCOLN'S PARENTAGE. ABRAHAM LINCOLN, An American Migration. By Marion D. Learned. *Illustrated.* Philadelphia, 1909. 8vo. ✛THE GENESIS OF LINCOLN. By James H. Cathey. (Washington, 1899). Square 12mo. ✛NANCY HANKS. By Caroline Hanks Hitchcock. New York, 1900. 16mo, Together three volumes, cloth.

Limited to 500 copies, signed. First editions of last two. Oakleaf 804; Fish 181, 418.

222. LINCOLN'S RELIGION. WAS ABRAHAM LINCOLN A SPIRITUALIST? By Mrs. Nettie C. Maynard. *Illustrated.* Philadelphia, 1891. 12mo, cloth. ✚ESSAY ON LINCOLN: Was He an Inspired Prophet? By M. R. Scott. Newark, Ohio, 1906. 12mo, cloth. ✚LINCOLN'S USE OF THE BIBLE. By S. Trevena Jackson. New York (1909). 16mo, wrappers. ✚A DEFENCE OF LINCOLN'S MOTHER, Conversion and Creed. Minneapolis, 1930. 12mo, wrappers. Together four volumes; first editions of first three. Fish 645 and Oakleaf 1249, 733.

223. LINCOLN ROMANCE. LINCOLN'S FIRST LOVE. By Carrie Douglas Wright. Chicago, 1901. 16mo. ✚SPANISH PEGGY, A Story of Young Illinois. By Mary Hartwell Catherwood. [*Illustrated*] New York, 1906. 8vo. Together two volumes, original cloth.
First editions. A.P.C. from Judd Stewart to Maj. Lambert, inscribed on fly leaf of second mentioned. Fine copies. Fish 1073 and Oakleaf 297.

224. LINCOLNIANA. LINCOLNIANA. In Memoriam. Boston, William V. Spencer, 1865. 4to, original cloth, beveled covers.
Limited to 250 copies. Without publisher's device at foot of the backstrip. Scarce. 3 A.L.S. laid in by F. E. Abbott, D. L. Hughes and J. Hazard Hartzell who are contributors to the book. Compiled by the publisher. Contains many sermons, eulogies, letters, etc. and a list of some 300 publications on Mr. Lincoln's death. Fish 593.

225. LINCOLNIANA. Another copy. 4to, original cloth, beveled covers.
Limited to 250 copies. With publisher's device at foot of backstrip. Scarce. Fish 593.

226. LINCOLNIANA. NEW YORK NEWS LETTER. Springfield, Ill., 1903. 4to. Lambert copy. Not in Fish or Oakleaf. ✚A LINCOLN SOUVENIR. [*Picture of desk*] The Leland Hotel, N. B. Wiggins. Springfield, no date. 8vo. Fish 1051. ✚THE LINCOLN WAY. Report of the Board of Trustees. Springfield, 1913. 8vo. Oakleaf 1400. Together three volumes, three-quarter morocco.

227. LINCOLN, SOLOMON. NOTES ON THE LINCOLN FAMILIES OF MASSACHUSETTS, with Some Account of the Family of Abraham Lincoln. Boston, 1865. Large 8vo, three-quarter straight grained morocco. Only 50 copies. A.L.S. re book to Hart. Hart, Lambert copy. Fish 595.

228. LODGE, HENRY CABOT. ADDRESS . . . On Abraham Lincoln. Boston, 1909. ✚ANOTHER COPY. Together two volumes, 4to, cloth.
First editions. A.P.C. of first to "Edward Everett Hale with the regards of Henry Cabot Lodge." T.L.S. by Lodge to Maj. Lambert tipped in second. Fish 874.

ORIGINAL MANUSCRIPT AND WASH DRAWINGS

229. LORD, JAMES JUDSON. AUTOGRAPH MANUSCRIPT SIGNED. "Lincoln Monument Dedicatory Poem." *Illustrated by W. Jerome*

Willoughby. ✝SAME. (Illinois Printing Company, Danville, Ill., 1907.) Together two volumes, 4to, cloth.
The original autograph manuscript with illustrations and the first book printing of it. A.L.S. by H. E. Barker gives history of the poem. Oakleaf 879.

230. (LOVEJOY, ELIJAH P.) NARRATIVE OF THE RIOTS AT ALTON: in Connection with the Death of Elijah P. Lovejoy. By Edward Beecher. Alton, 1838. 12mo, cloth. ✝MEMOIR OF THE REV. ELIJAH LOVEJOY, etc. By Joseph and Owen Lovejoy. New York, 1838. 12mo, cloth; rubbed, slightly shaken. ✝THE MARTYRDOM OF LOVEJOY. By an Eyewitness. Chicago, 1881. 8vo, cloth. Together three volumes.
First editions. First two mentioned very scarce. A.N.S. by Owen Lovejoy in second mentioned. Third is presentation copy from author with some facsimiles relating to the riots laid in. Interesting collection on an important incident in the history of free printing.

231. LOWELL, JAMES RUSSELL. AMONG MY BOOKS. Boston, 1870. ✝POLITICAL ESSAYS. Boston, 1888. ✝MY STUDY WINDOWS. Boston, 1872. Together three volumes, 12mo, original cloth, beveled covers; slightly rubbed at top and bottom of backstrips.
First editions of first two. Signature laid in: "J. R. Lowell. 1st March, 1871."

232. LUNT, GEORGE. THE ORIGIN OF THE LATE WAR. New York, 1866. 12mo, original cloth.
First edition. Autograph poem signed, 4 stanzas of 8 lines, tipped in. Not in Fish or Oakleaf.

233. McCARTHY, CHARLES H. LINCOLN'S PLAN OF RECONSTRUCTION. New York, 1901. Large 8vo, cloth, gilt top. First edition. Fish 612.

234. McCAULEY, JAS. A. CHARACTER AND SERVICES OF ABRAHAM LINCOLN. Baltimore, 1865. 8vo, three-quarter morocco. 500 copies. Two A.L.S. to Hart re book. Hart, Lambert copy. Fish 614.

235. McCLELLAN, GEN. G. B. LINCOLN'S TREATMENT OF GEN. GRANT . . . of Gen. McClellan. Fish 271. ✝McCLELLAN'S MILITARY CAREER. By Wm. Swinton. Oakleaf 1362. ✝"LEAVE POPE TO GET OUT OF HIS SCRAPE." 1862. (4 leaves) ✝TRIBUNE WAR TRACTS. No. 1. Report . . . Why M'Clellan was Removed. New York, 1863. Autograph of H. Ware. ✝McCLELLAN'S MILITARY CAREER. By Union Congressional Committee. Washington, 1864. Together five pamphlets, 8vo, printed wrappers.

236. McCLURE, A. K. ADDRESSES: Literary, Political, Legal and Miscellaneous. Two volumes. Philadelphia, 1894, 1895. Square 12mo, original cloth, unfaded; Volume I has few spots on front cover. First edition. A.P.C., signed by McClure, Jan. 29, 1904.

· **237. McCLURE, A. K.** LINCOLN AS POLITICIAN. Putnam, Conn., 1916. 8vo, wrappers.
Limited to 30 copies, by Tracy. A.L.S. by Barker laid in. Oakleaf 940.

238. MAGAZINE EXCERPTS. A collection of twelve articles by C. E. Carr, J. M. Davis, C. S. Taft, A. Cook, H. Garland, I. N. Arnold, C. King, E. A. Sikes, F. C. Payne and H. Watterson. 10 rebound in wrappers.

239. MARKENS, ISAAC. LINCOLN AND THE JEWS. Reprinted from Publications of the American Jewish Historical Society, No. 17, 1909. Large 8vo, three-quarter morocco. 200 copies. A.L.S. to Lambert. Limited edition with portrait mentioned by Oakleaf 915, as not issued. Lambert copy.

240. MARKENS, ISAAC. LINCOLN'S MASTERPIECE. New York, 1913. A.L.S. Limited to 100 copies. Oakleaf 918. ✚ABRAHAM LINCOLN AND THE JEWS. New York, 1909. Oakleaf 915. Together two pamphlets, 8vo, wrappers. Each A.P.C.

241. MARKHAM, EDWIN. LINCOLN and Other Poems. New York, 1901. 12mo, original cloth, gilt top, jacket.
First edition. A.L.S. by Markham to E. C. Stedman, 8vo, one page. Most unusual letter, reading in part: "I beg leave to ask for a few words of criticism and advice. Since early life poetry with me has been 'not a purpose, but a passion.' I enclose several bits of my verse—is it worth while for me to go on? . . ." From Stedman's library with his book plate. Fish 636.

241-A. MAURICE, ARTHUR B. THE HISTORY OF THE NINETEENTH CENTURY IN CARICATURE. [With] Frederic T. Cooper. *Profusely illustrated.* New York, 1904. Large 8vo, original cloth, gilt top.
First edition. Contains interesting chapter on Lincoln. Not in Fish or Oakleaf.

242. MELVILLE, HERMAN. BATTLE-PIECES and Aspects of the War. New York, 1866. 12mo, original green cloth; slightly rubbed.
First edition. Scarce. Judge McAdam's copy with autograph.

243. MEMORIALS. THE NATIONAL FAST DAY AND THE WAR. By Wm. A. Snively. Pittsburgh, 1863. ✚LEGISLATIVE HONORS to The Memory of President Lincoln. Message of Gov. Fenton. Albany, 1865. Rubbed. ✚MEMORIAL ADDRESS ON THE LIFE AND CHARACTER OF ABRAHAM LINCOLN. By George Bancroft. Washington, 1866. Fish 61. ✚REMINISCENCES OF THE LAST YEAR OF PRESIDENT LINCOLN'S LIFE. [*Two photographs laid in*] By Edw. D. Neill. St. Paul, 1885. Fish 683. Original wrappers bound in. Together four volumes, 8vo, original cloth.
First editions. Scarce. A.P.C. of first two and last mentioned.

244. MEMORIAL. MEMORIAL SERMON AND ADDRESS ON THE DEATH OF PRESIDENT LINCOLN, St. Andrews Church. Pittsburgh, 1865. 8vo, three-quarter morocco.
First edition. A.P.C. to E. M. Stanton. Contains Sermons by Wm. A. Snively and Wm. Preston. Burton Collection. Not in Fish or Oakleaf.

245. MEMORIALS. A Collection of twenty volumes of mostly memorials, by I. N. Arnold, Wm. H. Collins (A.N.), B. F. Morris,

J. C. Power, Republican Club, Union League, Philadelphia, Albion Lodge (Scarce), Centennial Association, Springfield, H. E. Hawley, Military Order of the Loyal Legion, and others. Fish 38, 214, 665, 764, 802, 986; Oakleaf 14, 63, 610 and 893.

246. MEMORIAL ADDRESSES. A Collection of nineteen Memorial Addresses, six A.P.C. Includes Fish 46 (500) and 736; Oakleaf 5, 223, 341, 342, 401, 1045, 1090 and 1180.

247. MEMORIAL. SENATE AND HOUSE OF THE UNITED STATES OF AMERICA. Buffalo, (1874). 8vo, 2 leaves. One of the earliest proposals to make Lincoln's birthday a legal holiday. Not in Fish or Oakleaf.

248. MESERVE, FREDERICK H. THE PHOTOGRAPHS OF LINCOLN. Prospectus with portrait. ✚A BRIEF SKETCH OF THE PHOTOGRAPHS OF LINCOLN. [With portrait] New York, the Quill Club, 1909. Together two pamphlets, 8vo, wrappers.

249. MISCEGENATION. WHAT MISCEGENATION IS. What We Are to Expect Now that Mr. Lincoln is Re-elected. By L. Seaman. New York, [1865]. Pictorial wrappers. Fish 844. ✚CAMPAIGN DOCUMENT, No. 11. Miscegenation Indorsed by the Republican Party. 2 leaves, unbound.. Not in Fish. Together two pamphlets, 8vo, scarce.

250. MISCELLANEOUS. ABRAHAM LINCOLN. By R. H. Stoddard. (1865). A.L.S. and D.S. Fish 898. ✚WASHINGTON AND LINCOLN. By David Swing. Lambert copy. Fish 925. ✚ABRAHAM LINCOLN. By C. J. Little. 1907. Lambert copy. Oakleaf 873. ✚THE ONE HUNDREDTH ANNIVERSARY. Issued by F. G. Blair. A.P.C. Oakleaf 701. ✚CENTENNIAL ANNIVERSARY . . . of the First Methodist Episcopal Church in Illinois. By M. H. Chamberlain. [1907] A.L.S., 6pp. Together five volumes, three-quarter morocco.

251. MISCELLANEOUS. A Collection of twelve volumes, including Washington in Lincoln's Time (Fish 141); Lincoln, by Markham (Fish 636); Wayside Glimpses, 1860; Liberty's Ordeal, by Bishop, 1864; Life of Andrew Johnson, by Moore, 1865; Canon Flashes, by Martenze, 1866; Lincoln Literary Collection, by McKaskey, 1897; etc. Various sizes, original cloth. First editions. Not in Fish or Oakleaf.

252. MITCHELL, WILLIAM. PERSONAL REMINISCENCES OF REV. WILLIAM MITCHELL . . . Incidents of Circuit Riding and Revival Work in the Early Days of Illinois. Arcola, Ill., 1897. 16mo, half cloth. A.P.C.

253. MITCHELL, S. S. IN MEMORIAM. Harrisburg, 1865. 8vo, three-quarter morocco. Scarce. Two A.L.S. to Hart re book. Hart, Lambert copy. Fish 658.

254. MONUMENTS. THE LINCOLN MONUMENT. Unveiled by Wallace Bruce at Edinburgh, Scotland. 1893. 12mo. Signed by Bissell, sculptor. A.L.S. by Bruce. Fish 302. ✚NATIONAL LINCOLN

MONUMENT. Official Programme. Springfield, Ill. 1874. Not in Fish. ✛SAME. Charter and Ordinances. 1901. Lambert copy. Not in Fish. ✛LINCOLN ANNIVERSARY. State of Nebraska. 1898. ✛LINCOLN GUARD OF HONOR. Springfield, 1880. Fish 722. Together five volumes, 8vo, half calf and three-quarter morocco.

255. MOREHOUSE, H. L. EVIL ITS OWN DESTROYER. East Saginaw, Mich., 1865. 12mo, three-quarter morocco. 1000 copies. A.L.S. to Hart re book. Hart, Lambert copy. Fish 663.

256. MORGAN, WILLIAM F. JOY DARKENED. Sermon Preached in St. Thomas' Church, New York, April 16th, 1865. 8vo, three-quarter morocco. 300 copies. A.P.C. to Hart. Lambert copy. Fish 664.

257. MYERS, LEONARD. ABRAHAM LINCOLN. A Memorial Address. Philadelphia, 1865. Three-quarter morocco. ✛SAME. Half calf. Together two volumes, 8vo.
First editions. A.P.C. to E. M. Stanton. Burton collection. Second is A.P.C. to C. K. Williams and autograph. Fish 674.

258. NELSON, HENRY A. THE DIVINELY PREPARED RULER, and the Fit End of Treason. Springfield, Ills., 1865. 8vo, three-quarter morocco. 250 copies. Lambert copy. Fish 684.

259. [NEWELL, R. H.] THE MARTYR PRESIDENT. New York, Carleton, Publisher, 1865. 12mo, half calf. 500 copies. Newell wrote under pseudonym of Orpheus C. Kerr. Lambert copy. Fish 640.

260. [NICOLAY, JOHN G.] JOURNAL OF ALFRED ELY, A Prisoner of War in Richmond. Edited by Charles Lanman. New York, 1862. 12mo, original cloth; backstrip faded, slightly shaken, library label.
First edition. This copy belonged to Nicolay, Lincoln's private secretary, and is inscribed on the inside front cover: "Jno. G. Nicolay Washington D. C., April 21st 1874."

261. NICOLAY, JOHN G. A SHORT LIFE OF ABRAHAM LINCOLN. New York, 1902. 8vo, original cloth, gilt top.
First edition. Envelope, addressed and signed by Nicolay laid in. Fish 700.

262. NORTON, ROBERT. MAPLE LEAVES FROM CANADA for the Grave of Abraham Lincoln. An Address by Robert F. Burns. St. Catherines, 1865. 12mo, half calf. 300 copies. Fish 632.

263. OAKLEAF, JOSEPH BENJAMIN. AN ANALYSIS OF THE GETTYSBURG ADDRESS. Moline, Ill., 1908. 12mo, cloth. 134 copies. Autographed. Oakleaf 1055.

264. OAKLEAF, JOSEPH BENJAMIN. ABRAHAM LINCOLN, His Friendship for Humanity and Sacrifice for Others. Augustana College, Rock Island, Ill. February 12, 1909. Small 4to, three-quarter morocco. A.P.C. to Little. T.L.S. laid in. Oakleaf 1056.

265. OAKLEAF, JOSEPH BENJAMIN. ABRAHAM LINCOLN, His Friendship for Humanity and Sacrifice for Others. Rock Island, Ill., 1909. 8vo, polished tan morocco, gilt stamped, dentelles, gilt edges, moiré doublures, boxed.
Limited to 50 copies, signed and presented to John S. Little. Two T.L.S. by Oakleaf re book, laid in.

266. OAKLEAF, JOSEPH BENJAMIN. LINCOLN BIBLIOGRAPHY, A List of Books and Pamphlets Relating to Abraham Lincoln. Cedar Rapids, Iowa, 1925. Large 8vo, three-quarter morocco, cloth, gilt top.
Limited to 102 copies, signed. Four T.L.S. by Oakleaf and correction slip laid in.

267. OFFICIAL. OFFICIAL PROCEEDINGS OF THE DEMOCRATIC CONVENTION, Held in 1864 at Chicago. Chicago, The Times Steam Book and Job Printing House, 1864. 8vo, unbound, stitched, 32 leaves. Rare. Not in Fish or Oakleaf. Fine copy.

268. OGLESBY, RICHARD J. MESSAGE TO THE GENERAL ASSEMBLY. Springfield, [Ills.], 1867. 8vo, original printed wrappers. A.L.S. re Lincoln.

269. OLDROYD, OSBORN H. WORDS OF LINCOLN. Washington, (1895). 12mo, original cloth.
First edition. Autographed. Superb copy, save binding on upside down. Fish 560.

270. OLDROYD, OSBORN H. THE ASSASSINATION OF ABRAHAM LINCOLN. Washington, 1901. 12mo, cloth. First edition. Fish 714.

271. OLDROYD, OSBORN H. THE OLDROYD LINCOLN MEMORIAL COLLECTION. Washington, D. C., 1903. 12mo, three-quarter morocco. Fish 715. ✚An Address, Delivered by Lincoln before the Springfield Washingtonian Temperance Society. Springfield, O. H. Oldroyd, 1889. 8vo, half calf. Fish 520. Together two volumes.

272. OLDROYD, OSBORN H. THE POETS' LINCOLN. *With many portraits of Lincoln, illustrations of events in his life, etc.* Washington, D. C., 1915. 8vo, half white buckram, cloth, gilt top, boxed.
Limited to 250 copies, signed by Oldroyd. Prospectus and 2 T.L.S. laid in. Oakleaf 1074.

273. OLD SALEM LINCOLN LEAGUE. LINCOLN AND NEW SALEM. Compiled by the Old Salem Lincoln League, Petersburg, Ill. [No imprint] Small 4to, original wrappers. Profusely illustrated.

274. ONSTOT, T. G. PIONEERS OF MENARD AND MASON COUNTIES. Forest City, Ill., 1902. 8vo, original cloth.
First edition. Cover title "Lincoln and Salem." Fine copy. Fish says: "Deliciously artless and not very accurate, but worthy of a place in Lincoln collections." Fish 720.

275. PAMPHLETS. A Collection of forty pamphlets on Lincoln, Centenary memorials, Addresses, Programmes, Speeches, Newspapers, etc. Some A.P.C.

276. PAMPHLETS. A Collection of thirty-seven pamphlets on Lincoln, Transactions of Historical Societies, Memorials, Eulogies, etc. Some A.P.C.

277. PATTERSON, ADONIRAM J. Eulogy on Abraham Lincoln. Portsmouth [N. H.], 1865. 8vo, half cloth. 1000 copies. A.P.C. Fish 732.

278. PATTON, A. S. The Nation's Loss and Its Lessons. An Occasional Discourse on the Assassination of President Lincoln. Utica, N. Y., 1865. 8vo, three-quarter morocco. 500 copies. A.L.S. re pamphlet; also envelope addressed to Hart. The Hart, Lambert, McAleenan copy. Fish 735.

279. PECK, GEORGE R. Abraham Lincoln. Marquette Club, Chicago, February 12th, 1895. 4to, three-quarter morocco. Privately printed. Book plate of Wm. Carey. Lambert copy. Fish 737.

280. PECKHAM, JAMES. Gen. Nathaniel Lyon, and Missouri in 1860. New York, 1866. 12mo, original cloth.
First edition. A little known and scarce Lincoln item. Contains twelve articles, 1860, urging Lincoln's election. Not in Fish or Oakleaf.

281. PITMAN, BENN. The Assassination of President Lincoln and the Trial of the Conspirators. New York, 1865. 8vo, cloth; backstrip rubbed. First edition. Fish 752.

282. POETRY ON LINCOLN. Sir Copp. By Thomas Clarke. Chicago, 1866. ✛Patriotic Poems. By Francis de Haes Janvier. Philadelphia, 1866. ✛Verses of Many Days. By William O. Stoddard. New York, 1875. ✛Bugle-Echoes. Edited by Francis F. Browne. *Illustrated.* New York, 1886. Together four volumes, 12mo, cloth.
First editions of first three. First mentioned devoted to assassination. A.P.C. of third mentioned. None in Fish or Oakleaf.

283. PORTRAITS and Sketches of the Lives of All the Candidates for the Presidency and Vice-Presidency, for 1860. New York, 1860. 8vo, original printed wrappers. Eight fine portraits engraved on steel. Scarce. Fish 756.

284. POST, JACOB. Discourse on the Assassination of President Lincoln, Preached in Camp, at Harrison's Landing, Va. Oswego, 1865. 8vo, three-quarter morocco. 500 copies. A.L.S. to Hart re book. Hart, Lambert copy. Fish 757.

285. POTTER, WILLIAM J. THE NATIONAL TRAGEDY: Four Sermons . . . on the Life and Death of Abraham Lincoln. New Bedford, Mass., 1865. 8vo, three-quarter morocco. 500 copies. A.L.S. to Hart re book. Hart, Lambert copy. Fish 758.

286. PRATT, SILAS G. LINCOLN IN STORY. Tokio [Japan], 1904. 12mo, half calf. In English, but Japanese characters on title and page 165. Oakleaf 1124.

287. PRESIDENT LINCOLN'S SPEECH AT GETTYSBURG, November 19, 1863. [By S. A. Green] 8vo, 2 leaves; edges rubbed. Very scarce. Less than 50 published. Fish 770.

288. PRESIDENTIAL ADDRESSES. ABRAHAM LINCOLN. An Address by William McKinley of Ohio. Before the Marquette Club, Chicago, 1896. Fish 627. ✦ADDRESS OF PRESIDENT ROOSEVELT on the occasion of the Celebration of the Hundredth Anniversary of the Birth of Lincoln. Hodgenville, Ky. Washington, 1909. Oakleaf 1208. Together two volumes, 8vo, three-quarter morocco. Lambert copies.

289. PRESIDENTIAL BIOGRAPHY. ACROSTICAL PEN PORTRAITS of the Eighteen Presidents of the United States. By D. F. Lockerby. Philadelphia, 1876. 12mo, cloth. ✦THE LIVES AND GRAVES OF OUR PRESIDENTS. By G. S. Weaver. Chicago, (1883). 8vo, padded leather, gilt edges. ✦OUR MARTYR PRESIDENTS. By John Coulter. No place, (1901). 8vo, cloth. ✦THE PRESIDENTS OF THE UNITED STATES. By J. C. Abbott and R. H. Conwell. Portland, [1884]. Thick 8vo, cloth. ✦PRESIDENTS OF THE UNITED STATES. *Steel portraits with facsimile autographs.* 12mo, rubbed leather folder. Together five volumes.
First editions of first three. Scarce. None of this lot mentioned in Fish or Oakleaf.

290. PUTNAM, GEORGE. CITY DOCUMENT. No. 5. An Address Delivered before the City Government. Roxbury, [Mass.] 1865. 8vo, three-quarter morocco. 1000 copies. A.L.S. to Hart. Very rare original Order of Services on the day of the Address laid in. Hart, Lambert copy. Fish 780.

291. RANKIN, HENRY B. PERSONAL RECOLLECTIONS OF ABRAHAM LINCOLN. *With portraits.* New York, 1916. 8vo, cloth. ✦INTIMATE CHARACTER SKETCHES OF ABRAHAM LINCOLN. Philadelphia, 1924. 8vo, cloth. ✦OUR FIRST AMERICAN. Springfield, 1915. 4to, wrappers. ✦LINCOLN'S COOPER INSTITUTE SPEECH. (Springfield), 1917. 16mo, wrappers. Together four pieces, each inscribed by Rankin, Lincoln's Sangamon friend and law student. Oakleaf 1141, 1144, 1140 and 1142.

292. RANKIN, J. E. MOSES AND JOSHUA. Preached in the Winthrop Church, Charlestown, Boston, 1865. 8vo, three-quarter morocco. 700 copies. A.L.S. to Hart, re book. Lambert copy. Fish 785.

293. RECOLLECTIONS. PERSONAL RECOLLECTIONS OF ABRAHAM LINCOLN and the Civil War. By James R. Gilmore. *Illustrated.*

Boston, 1898. 8vo. Fish 347. ✠ABRAHAM LINCOLN. By Carl Schurz. Boston, 1892. 12mo. Fish 839. ✠FIFTY YEARS OF PUBLIC SERVICE. By Shelby M. Cullom. *With portraits.* Chicago, 1911. 8vo. Together three volumes, original cloth, two jackets.

First editions. A.L.S. and receipt, signed by Gilmore. A.L.S. by Schurz. T.L.S. by Cullom.

294. RECOLLECTIONS. RECOLLECTIONS OF LINCOLN. By J. O. Cunningham. [Reprinted from the Bibliotheca Sacra, October, 1908] A. C. Lambert copy. Oakleaf 408. ✠PERSONAL REMINISCENCES OF ABRAHAM LINCOLN. By Dr. William Jayne. [Springfield, 1907] A. C. Oakleaf 739. ✠PERSONAL RECOLLECTIONS OF ABRAHAM LINCOLN. By Gen. O. O. Howard. [Excerpt from Century April 1908] A.L.S. Together three volumes, 8vo, three-quarter morocco.

295. RECONSTRUCTION. A Collection of 28 Pamphlets on Reconstruction, bound for E. M. Stanton. 1866-68. Thick 8vo, three-quarter morocco, boards; worn, shaken.

First editions, containing many scarce pamphlets, such as: "War' of Races. By J. H. Gilmer. Richmond, 1867."; and "Roll of the Black Dupes and White Renegades who Voted in Mobile for the Menagerie Constitution for Alabama. Mobile, 1868." A.P.C. to E. M. Stanton, Sect'y of War under Lincoln, of pamphlets by C. G. Loring and Cleveland Convention. J. E. Burton inscribed on end paper: "Paid Guy Nichols $21.00 From Library of Secretary of War, etc."

296. REED, V. D. THE CONFLICT OF TRUTH. A Sermon, etc. Camden, N. J., 1865. 8vo, three-quarter morocco. 500 copies. Portrait and two A.L.S. to Hart re book. Hart, Lambert, McAleenan copy. Fish 795.

297. REPUBLICAN CLUB OF NEW YORK. ADDRESSES Delivered at the Lincoln Dinners of the Republican Club of New York in Response to the Toast Abraham Lincoln, 1887-1909. Privately printed, 1909. 8vo, three-quarter brown morocco, boards, gilt top. 500 copies, signed. Burton collection. Oakleaf 1161.

298. REPUBLICAN CLUB OF NEW YORK. ABRAHAM LINCOLN'S LOST SPEECH, May 29, 1856. A Souvenir of the Eleventh Annual Lincoln Dinner of the Republican Club of New York, at the Waldorf, Feb. 12, 1897. New York, 1897. 8vo, original white cloth, gilt top.

Limited to 500 copies. A.L.S. tipped in by Judd Stewart to Maj. Lambert, 3 pages, 12mo, "Mch 8-08." Magnificent letter, referring to their collecting activities and to this book which Stewart gave Lambert. Handsome engraved book plate of Stewart. Unusual association copy. Fish 802.

299. RICE, DANIEL. THE PRESIDENT'S DEATH—Its Import. [Lafayette, 1865] 8vo, three-quarter morocco. 1000 copies. A.L.S. to Hart re book and other authors. Hart, Lambert copy. Fish 810.

300. RITCHIE, GEORGE THOMAS. A LIST OF LINCOLNIANA in the Library of Congress. Washington, 1903. ✠SAME. Revised edition with Supplement. Washington, 1906. Unopened. Together two volumes, 4to, original cloth.

First and second editions, respectively. Fish 813.

SECOND SESSION
Thursday Evening, June 15, 8 p.m.

301. ROGERS, J. W. MADAME SURRATT; A Drama in Five Acts. Washington, D. C., 1879. 16mo, three-quarter morocco, original wrappers bound in. Very scarce. A.P.C. to Senator Roscoe Conkling. Fish 818.

302. ROTHSCHILD, ALONZO. LINCOLN, Master of Men, A Study in Character. *With portraits.* Boston, 1906. Large 8vo, original cloth, paper label, jacket.
Limited to 150 copies, bound uncut with paper label. A most important addition to Lincoln biography. Fish 820.

303. ROTHSCHILD, ALONZO. "HONEST ABE," A Study of Integrity, Based on the Early Life of Abraham Lincoln. Boston, 1917. Half cloth, boards, jacket, unopened. ✢SAME. Cloth. Together two volumes, 8vo.
Limited to 330 copies of first. First trade edition, first issue of second. A.L.S. by Rothschild re Lincoln. Judge Roger's copy, with autograph. Oakleaf 1218, 1217.

304. SALE CATALOGUES. LIBRARY OF MAJOR WM. B. LAMBERT. 1914. Half calf. Priced. ✢ANOTHER COPY. Two parts. ✢THE FINE LIBRARY OF JOHN E. BURTON. Parts I and VI, Lincolniana. 1915. Partly priced. ✢THE LINCOLN COLLECTION OF EMANUEL HERTZ. 1927. Together six volumes, 8vo, original wrappers.

305. SALE CATALOGUES. A Collection of eight catalogues on Lincoln, including Merwin-Clayton Sales, Geo. D. Smith, Anderson Galleries (Burton collection), Heartman (Lambert material), Chicago Public Library and Albert H. Griffith (A.P.C.).

306. SANDBURG, CARL. ABRAHAM LINCOLN, the Prairie Years. *With 105 illustrations from photographs, and many cartoons, sketches, maps and letters.* Two volumes. New York, (1928). 8vo, three-quarter morocco, boards, gilt tops. Autographed.

307. SCRAP BOOK. Early scrap book of Lincoln interest, containing contemporary newspaper reports of his great Cooper Union speech, his speech on the shoe strike in Mass., speeches of Seward, Doolittle, Wade, etc. 8vo, half calf; rubbed.

LAMBERT COPY WITH BOTH CHICAGO AND NEW YORK IMPRINTS. SCRIPPS A.L.S. BOUND IN

308. [SCRIPPS, JOHN LOCKE] LIFE OF ABRAHAM LINCOLN. Chicago Press and Tribune Co., 1860. Also bound in is: Tribune Tracts. No. 6. LIFE OF ABRAHAM LINCOLN. New York, Horace Greeley & Co., 1860. 8vo, three-quarter green morocco, marbled boards, gilt top in green morocco solander case, inner cloth wrapper.

First edition. The excessively rare Chicago imprint of which only a few copies are known to exist, together with the rare New York imprint which, according to a letter of Scripps' in the Introduction to the reprint of his biography in 1900, were issued simultaneously. Advertising matter on page 32 of first mentioned begins: "The Chicago Press and Tribune. Campaign, of 1860." Laid in is A.N.S. by Lincoln: "Hon. J. R. Doolittle please call and see me this morning. A. Lincoln. March 24, 1864." Verso: "16· N. A. St. at Del. ave. & 1st St. E." Tipped in is A.L.S. by Scripps, 4to, 4 pages, to his sister, dated: "June 19th 1841." This is the third known biography of Lincoln; used for campaign purposes. The proof was read, corrected and authorized by Lincoln personally. When the advance sheets reached Lincoln, he is supposed to have summoned Mr. Scripps and said to him: "That paragraph wherein you state I read Plutarch's Lives was not true when you wrote it, but I want your book, even if it is nothing more than a campaign sketch, to be faithful to the facts, and in order that that statement might be literally true, I secured the book a few days ago and have just read it through." Lambert copy. Fish 842.

309. [SCRIPPS, JOHN LOCKE] Tribune Tracts. No. 6. LIFE OF ABRAHAM LINCOLN. New York, Horace Greeley, 1860. 8vo, unbound. Fine copy. Fish 842.

310. [SCRIPPS, JOHN LOCKE] SAME. New York, Horace Greeley, 1860. 8vo, cloth. Fish 842.

311. [SCRIPPS, JOHN LOCKE] SAME. 8vo, full calf, morocco labels. The John E. Burton copy. Fish 842.

312. SCRIPPS, JOHN LOCKE. THE FIRST PUBLISHED LIFE OF ABRAHAM LINCOLN. Reprinted in 1900, by The Cranbrook Press. Folio, three-quarter vellum, boards. ✠TRANSACTIONS OF THE ILLINOIS STATE HISTORICAL SOCIETY. (Springfield, 1924.) 8vo, cloth. Together two volumes.

Limited to 245 copies of first mentioned. Edited by Scripps' daughter, Grace L. Scripps Dyche, with her A.L.S. re book. Burton copy with book plate. Various T.L.S. and D.S. relating to book. Fish 843. Second mentioned contains an article by Mrs. Dyche on J. L. Scripps, with illustrations.

313. SEARING, EDWARD. PRESIDENT LINCOLN IN HISTORY. An Address Delivered in . . . Milton, Wis. Janesville, 1865. 8vo, three-quarter morocco. 300 copies. Two A.L.S. to Hart re book and other authors. Hart, Lambert copy. Fish 845.

314. SERMONS. A Collection of six A.P.C. Funeral Sermons by A. H. Bullock (2500), Daniel Clark (1000), Elias Nason (1000), R. S. Storrs (1500), M.ⱼ C. Sutphen (750) and A. A. E. Taylor (1000). 8vo, wrappers. Fish 151, 203, 677, 907, 921 and 935.

315. SERMONS. A Collection of seven A.P.C. Funeral Sermons by C. M. Moore (750), J. G. Butler (2500), D. Clark (1000), H. P. Crozier (1000), R. Eddy (300), W. R. Gordon (800), and G. Haven (500). 8vo, wrappers. Fish 163, 165, 203, 236, 297, 354 and 398 respectively.

316. SIMPSON, MATTHEW. FUNERAL ADDRESS Delivered at the Burial of President Lincoln at Springfield, Ill. New York, 1865. 16mo, three-quarter morocco. 2000 copies. Lambert copy. Fish 859.

317. SLAVERY. LETTER ON THE RELATION OF THE WHITE AND AFRICAN RACES. [By James Mitchell] Washington, 1862. Fish 657 ("Probably drawn up at Lincoln's request."). ✚ABOLITION AND SECESSION. By a Unionist. N. Y., 1862. ✚LOYAL PUBLICATION SOCIETY, Nos. 26, 36 and 50. By A. J. Hamilton (Fish 379), A. H. Stephens and J. A. Hamilton. Together five pamphlets, 8vo, wrappers.

318. SNODGRASS, WINFIELD C. ABRAHAM LINCOLN, the Typical American. Plainfield, N. J., February 12, 1905. 4to, three-quarter morocco.
Limited to 50 copies printed for private circulation by Judd Stewart. Illustrated with portrait and 2 views. A.P.C. to Maj. Lambert from Stewart. Fish 871.

319. SNODGRASS, WINFIELD C. ABRAHAM LINCOLN, The Typical American, A Sermon. Preached in the First Methodist Episcopal Church, Plainfield, N. J., February 12, 1905. 4to, full brown morocco, red and blue labels.
Limited to 50 copies printed for private circulation by Judd Stewart. Burton collection. Fish 871.

320. SONG BOOKS. THE NEW YANKEE DOODLE. By Dan (Not Bev) Tucker. Washington, 1861. 12mo; front wrapper lacking. ✚TOUCH THE ELBOW SONGSTER. New. . . . Patriotic Army Songs. New York, (1862). 16mo. Together two pamphlets, original printed wrappers. Not in Fish or Oakleaf.

321. SOUVENIR. SOUVENIR OF LINCOLN'S BIRTHPLACE. Issued by Thos. B. Kirkpatrick. Hodgensville (sic), Ky. [*Illustrations*] No place, 1903. Oblong 8vo, three-quarter morocco. T. L. re Lincoln farm. Lambert copy. Fish 873.

322. SOUVENIR POSTAL CARDS. A Collection of 172 postal cards of Lincolniana, some addressed to Lambert, Stewart, etc.

323. SPEAR, SAMUEL T. THE PUNISHMENT OF TREASON. Brooklyn, 1865. 8vo, three-quarter morocco. 3000 copies. A.L.S. to Hart re book. Hart, Lambert copy. Fish 876.

324. SPEED, JAMES. ADDRESS before the Loyal Legion, at Cincinnati, May 4, 1887, on Abraham Lincoln. Louisville, 1888. 8vo, three-quarter calf, boards. Burton collection. Fish 880.

325. SPEED, JOSHUA F. REMINISCENCES OF ABRAHAM LINCOLN and Notes of a Visit to California. Louisville, Ky., 1884. 8vo, three-quarter morocco, boards.

First edition. An account written by one of Lincoln's earliest and most intimate friends. Fish 881.

326. STARR, FREDERICK JR. THE MARTYR PRESIDENT. St. Louis, 1865. 8vo, three-quarter morocco. A.L.S. to Hart re book. Hart, Lambert copy. Fish 889.

327. STARR, JOHN W. LINCOLN AND THE RAILROADS. *Illustrated.* New York, 1927. Large 8vo, cloth, unopened, boxed.

Limited to 287 copies, signed. Fine.

328. STEELE, RICHARD H. VICTORY AND MOURNING. New Brunswick, N. J., 1865. 8vo, half calf. 1000 copies. A.P.C. Lambert copy. Fish 890.

329. STEPHENS, ALEXANDER H. A COMPENDIUM OF THE HISTORY OF THE UNITED STATES. From the Earliest Settlements to 1872. New York, 1880. 12mo, half morocco, cloth; rubbed, fly leaf lacking, some pencil erasures.

Autograph presentation copy, inscribed on the fly leaf: "To Emmett Robertson Cax, as a birthday present with the kind regards and best wishes of Alexander Stephens. National Hotel Washington D.C. 23 December 1880." Stephens, who became vice-president of the confederacy, befriended Lincoln in his first congressional term, 1847-9.

330. STEVENS, FRANK E. THE BLACK HAWK WAR. *Illustrated with upward of three hundred rare and interesting portraits and views.* Chicago, 1903. Narrow 4to, cloth, paper label, gilt top.

First edition, limited. Contains author's MS. notes. A.L.S. by Stevens and prospectus laid in. Not in Fish or Oakleaf.

331. STEWART, DANIEL. OUR NATIONAL SORROW. Johnstown [N. Y.], 1865. 8vo, three-quarter morocco. 500 copies. A.L.S. to Hart re book. Hart, Lambert copy. Fish 897.

332. STEWART, JUDD. LINCOLN AND THE NEW YORK HERALD TRIBUNE. Unpublished Letters of Abraham Lincoln from the Collection of Judd Stewart. Plainfield, N. J., Privately printed, 1907. 8vo, half cloth, boards.

Limited to 100 copies. Letters in facsimile. Several T.L.S. relating to the book laid in. Oakleaf 1339.

333. STEWART, JUDD. SOME LINCOLN CORRESPONDENCE WITH SOUTHERN LEADERS before the Outbreak of the Civil War. From the Collection of Judd Stewart, 1909. 8vo, three-quarter morocco. A.P.C. and A.L.S. to Maj. Lambert re how to collect. Lambert copy. Oakleaf 1340.

334. STONE, ANDREW L. A DISCOURSE . . . ON ABRAHAM LINCOLN . . . Preached in Park Street Church, Boston. Boston, J. K. Wiggins, 1865. 300 copies. Burton collection. Fish 906.

335. STORRS, RICHARD S. An Oration Commemorative of Abraham Lincoln. Brooklyn, 1865. 8vo, half calf. 1500 copies. A.P.C. to Hart. Hart, Lambert copy. Fish 907.

336. STOWE, HARRIET BEECHER. Men of Our Times. *Beautifully illustrated with eighteen steel portraits.* Hartford, 1868. Rubbed, front hinge split. ✛OLDROYD, OSBORN H. The Lincoln Memorial: Album-Immortelles. New York, 1883. Together two volumes, 8vo, calf.
First edition of first. A.P.C. of second. Fish 908, 711.

337. SUMNER, CHARLES. Emancipation! Its Policy and Necessity as a War Measure for the Suppression of the Rebellion. Faneuil Hall, Oct. 6, 1862. 8vo, stitched, 10 leaves. A.N.S. laid in. Very scarce. Not in Fish or Oakleaf.

338. SUTLIFF, MARY LOUISA. Bibliography of Poems Relating to Abraham Lincoln. Albany, 1893. 4to, half cloth, boards.
Typed copy of the original manuscript in the State Library at Albany which was never published. Unique item.

339. SWAIN, LEONARD. A Nation's Sorrow. [Providence (?), 1865] Tall 8vo, three-quarter morocco. 1000 copies. A.L.S. to Hart re book. Hart, Lambert copy. Fish 922.

340. SWEESTER, SETH. A Commemorative Discourse on the Death of Abraham Lincoln. Worcester, Mass., 1865. 8vo, three-quarter morocco. 600 copies. A.L.S., 4pp., to Hart, saying he could not supply the demand. Hart, Lambert copy. Fish 923.

341. [SYLVAIN, LEO] Les Contemporains. [*Portrait*] Lincoln (1809-1865). Les Contemporains 105. 4to, title on wrappers. Scarce. Page 15 has full page cut of assassination scene. Oakleaf 1363.

342. TAPLEY, RUFUS T. Eulogy of Abraham Lincoln. At Saco, Maine. Biddeford, 1865. 8vo, three-quarter morocco. 1500 copies. A.P.C. to Hart. Hart, Lambert copy. Fish 929.

343. TARBELL, IDA M. The Early Life of Abraham Lincoln. Assisted by J. McCan Davis. *With 160 illustrations, including 20 portraits of Lincoln.* New York, S. S. McClure, 1896. Large 8vo, original wrappers. First edition. Fish 932.

ONE OF 25 SETS

344. TARBELL, IDA M. The Life of Abraham Lincoln. *Illustrated.* Two volumes. New York, 1900. 4to, half buckram, boards.
Limited to 25 sets, signed. Miss Tarbell's biography brought to light much important new material. Fish 933.

345. TARBELL, IDA M. He Knew Lincoln. [*Illustrated*] New York, 1907. 12mo, original cloth. ✛THE AMERICAN MAGAZINE.

New York, February, 1907. 8vo, original wrappers. Together two volumes.

First edition of first mentioned. Autograph of Ida M. Tarbell on fly leaf. A.L.S. by Barker laid in. Oakleaf 1376. First appearance of "He Knew Lincoln" in second mentioned.

346. TARBELL, IDA M. He Knew Lincoln. Also: A Talk about Lincoln. [Anonymous] [Excerpts from the American Magazine, February, 1907] 4to, three-quarter morocco.
The Lambert copy, "Inscribed for John S. Little by Ida M. Tarbell. Souvenir of a delightful visit, December 2—1928." A.L.S. to Maj. Lambert, 2pp. making inquiry about the owner of Lincoln's exercise book and asking permission, if it is Maj. Lambert, to reproduce it in her book.

347. THOMPSON, MAURICE. Lincoln's Grave. Cambridge, Stone and Kimball, 1894. 16mo, vellum, silk ties. 450 copies of the first edition. Fish 955.

348. THOMPSON, RICHARD W. Personal Recollections of Sixteen Presidents, From Washington to Lincoln. [*Illustrated with portraits*] Two volumes. Indianapolis, 1894. 8vo, cloth, gilt tops.
Edition de Luxe. Very fine set. Not in Fish or Oakleaf.

349. [TORREY, HIRAM D.] The Tragedy of Abraham Lincoln. By an American Artist. Glasgow, 1876. 12mo, three-quarter straight grained morocco. This edition has no copyright notice on verso of title. Very scarce. A.P.C. Lambert copy. Fish 963.

350. TRIAL Of the Assassins and Conspirators for the Murder of Abraham Lincoln. *Correct likenesses and graphic history of all the assassins, etc.* Philadelphia, (1864, sic). 8vo, pictorial wrappers; backstrip damaged. Fish 968.

351. TRIBUTES. Patriotism in Poetry and Prose: Being Selected Passages from J. E. Murdoch, etc. Philadelphia, 1864. 12mo. ✢Poetical Tributes to the Memory of Abraham Lincoln. Philadelphia, 1865. 12mo. ✢The Book of Lincoln. Compiled by Mary Wright-Davis. *Illustrated.* New York, (1919). 8vo. Together three volumes, cloth.
First editions. A.P.C. of first mentioned. Not in Fish or Oakleaf. Last two Fish 753 (compiled by J. N. Plotts) and Oakleaf 423.

LARGE PAPER EDITION

352. TRIBUTES. Tributes to the Memory of Abraham Lincoln. *Reproduction in facsimile of eighty-seven memorials,* Addressed by Foreign Municipalities and Societies to the Government of the United States. Washington, 1885. Elephant folio, full morocco, gilt dentelles and edges, moiré silk doublures.
Very rare large paper edition in facsimile. Contains 92 listed plates, instead of the 87 mentioned on the title. Sumptuously printed and bound. Fish 994.

353. TUCKER, J. T. A Discourse. Holliston, [Mass.] 1865. 8vo, wrappers. 500 copies. A.P.C. Fish 971.

354. UMSTEAD, JUSTUS T. A Discourse on the Death of President Lincoln. West Chester, 1865. 8vo, three-quarter morocco. 500 copies. A.L.S. to Hart re book. Hart, Lambert, McAleenan copy. Fish 978.

355. UNION LEAGUE CLUB. The Annual Dinner of the Union League Club of Brooklyn. February 12, 1908. *Portraits from the Frederick Hill Meserve Collection.* New York, 1908. 12mo, three-quarter morocco.

Contains 5 photographs pasted in, 3 of them from the original Brady negatives, the first being from the famous ambrotype owned by Lambert. Oakleaf 1422.

356. VINCENT, MARVIN R. A Sermon on the Assassination of Abraham Lincoln. Troy, 1865. 8vo, three-quarter morocco. First edition. 2000 copies. A.L.S. to Hart re book. Hart, Lambert copy. Fish 1009.

357. VINCENT, THOMAS M. Military Order of the Loyal Legion. War Papers. 8. Abraham Lincoln and Edwin M. Stanton. No place, [1892]. 8vo, three-quarter morocco. A.P.C. Fish 1011.

358. VOLK, LEONARD W. The Lincoln Life-Mask and How it Was Made. Reprinted from the Century Magazine for December, 1881. 4to. A.L.S. to Col. Whitney re Lincoln. ✛The Lincoln Life Mask, Hands, Bust and Statuette. Published by C. Hennecke Co., Milwaukee, [1891]. Oblong 12mo. T.L. to Lambert. Fish 583. Together two volumes, three-quarter morocco.

359. WALL, BERNHARDT. The Gettysburg Speech by Abraham Lincoln. Delivered on Nov. 19, 1863. New York, Etched by Bernhardt Wall, 1924. 4to, half cloth, boards.

Limited to 100 copies of the first printing, signed. Twenty leaves of text and pictures, etched, printed and bound by Wall, on hand made paper. Prospectus and A.L.S. laid in. Oakleaf 1447.

360. WARD, THOMAS. War Lyrics. New York, no date. 12mo, half calf. A.P.C. to Gen. Viele. Not in Fish or Oakleaf.

361. WATTERSON, HENRY. Abraham Lincoln. Chicago, Feb. 12, 1895. 4to, wrappers. A.L.S. Fish 1027, save copyright 1899.

362. WEBB, EDWIN B. Memorial Sermons. Boston, 1865. 8vo, half calf. 1000 copies. A.P.C. Lambert copy. Fish 1029.

363. WEIK, JESSE W. Lincoln as a Lawyer, With an Account of his First Case. [Excerpt from Century, June 1904] 4to, three-quarter morocco. A.L.S. to Lambert. Lambert copy.

364. WEIK, JESSE W. Lincoln's Vote for Vice-President, in the Philadelphia Convention of 1856. [Excerpt from Century Magazine, June, 1908] Large 8vo, three-quarter morocco. A.L.S. to Lambert.

365. WEIK, JESSE W. The Real Lincoln. Boston, 1922. 8vo, cloth, jacket. ✚Abraham Lincoln. [With] Wm. H. Herndon. Two volumes. New York, 1896. 12mo, cloth. Together three volumes.
First edition of first. A.P.C. by Weik to J. S. Little. Oakleaf 1467 and Fish 410.

366. [WESTCOTT, T.] Chronicles of the Great Rebellion against the United States. Philadelphia (1866). 8vo, original cloth.
First edition. Very scarce. Contains Lincoln material not published elsewhere. A.P.C., inscribed on fly leaf. Not in Fish or Oakleaf.

367. WHIPPLE, WAYNE. The Story-Life of Lincoln. *Illustrated.* Philadelphia, (1908). 8vo, cloth, gilt top.
Limited to 800 copies of the Memorial Edition of the 100th Birthday of Lincoln. Book plate, menu and 2 A.L.S. of Lincoln Centennial Association laid in. Superb copy. Oakleaf 1477.

368. WHITE, PLINY H. A Sermon, Occasioned by the Assassination of Abraham Lincoln . . . Preached at Coventry, Vt. Brattleboro, 1865. 8vo, three-quarter morocco. 150 copies. A.L.S. to Hart re book. Very scarce. Hart, Lambert copy. Fish 1039.

369. [WHITE, RICHARD GRANT] The New Gospel of Peace, According to St. Benjamin. Sinclair Tousey, 121 Nassau Street, New York [1863]. ✚Same. Book Second. New York: Sinclair Tousey, Publisher, No. 121 Nassau Street. [1863]. ✚Same. Book Third. American News Agency: 113 & 121 Nassau Street, New York, [1864]. Wrappers not glazed. ✚Same. Book Fourth and Last. New York, The American News Company, 119 & 121 Nassau Street [1866]. ✚Revelations: A Companion to the "New Gospel of Peace." According to Abraham. New York, Published by M. Doolady, 1863. Creased through centre. Together five pamphlets, 12mo, original glazed wrappers, in half morocco, cloth slip case, inner cloth folder.
First edition in original parts of "The New Gospel" which deals generally with the events of Lincoln's administration from 1863 onward, in a brilliant vein of wit and satire. Superb copies of Oakleaf 1020, 1021, 1022, 1023. "Revelations" is an anonymous pamphlet denouncing the Patriarch (Lincoln), his administration, etc. Fish 805, save that the imprints on the cover and title page are identical.

370. [WHITE, RICHARD GRANT] The New Gospel of Peace, According to St. Benjamin. New York, The American News Company, 119 & 121 Nassau Street, 1866. 12mo, three-quarter brown morocco, boards, in half morocco, cloth slip case, inner cloth wrapper.
First collected edition. The author's own copy with his MS. notes, giving the originals of the allegoric characters; e.g. Sheik Ahgo has "Chicago" in the margin. Two A.L.S. Oakleaf 1024.

371. WHITING, WILLIAM. The War Powers of the President. Third edition. Boston, 1863. 8vo, original wrappers, slightly stained. A.P.C. to Thaddeus Stevens. Fish 1040.

372. WHITMAN, WALT. Specimen Days. & collect. Philadelphia, Rees Welsh & Co., 1882-'83. Original cloth. ✚Memories of President

LINCOLN and Other Lyrics of the War. Portland, Thomas B. Mosher, 1906. Boards, boxed. Together two volumes, 12mo.

First edition. First issue of first mentioned. Limited to 100 copies on Japan vellum of second mentioned.

IMMACULATE COPY IN ORIGINAL JACKET WITH A.L.S.

373. WHITNEY, HENRY C. LIFE ON THE CIRCUIT WITH LINCOLN. *Illustrated.* Boston (1892). 4to, original cloth, gilt top, jacket.

First edition. Superb copy of this great Lincoln rarity. Autograph letter signed, 8vo, 2 pages, to Geo. B. Ayres laid in: "No one now on earth knows how Abraham Lincoln looked before he became President better than I do. I was a young man in those early days; I admired Lincoln and believed in him. I slept with him, walked with him and saw him in all his moods and tenses . . . No one of his close friends ever liked the whiskers. Had he tried wearing them 'on the Circuit' we would not have tolerated it. All of the old set who were Lincoln's companions and may still live will concur with me in what I say concerning the wonderful fidelity of your picture. . . . When Herndon was getting up his 'Life of Lincoln' I sent him a copy from this same negative, and he chose this likeness as the best of all for his book . . ." Fish 1048. Vide No. 411.

EARLIEST KNOWN BIOGRAPHY

374. WIGWAM BIOGRAPHY. THE LIFE, SPEECHES AND PUBLIC SERVICES OF ABRAHAM LINCOLN. Together with a Sketch of the Life of Hannibal Hamlin. New York, Rudd & Carleton, 1860. 7⅜" x 4⅜", three-quarter morocco; front wrapper mended through centre. Contents superb.

"The Wigwam Edition." Rare. T.L.S. by Newhall to Little says this is the tallest copy he has ever seen, and has the back wrapper which is usually missing. "I consider this much rarer than the Scripps." Earliest known biography of Lincoln, being copyrighted June 8. Fish says: "The unknown author apparently did not know the true name of his subject, yet he boldly traced 'Abram's' genealogy to the Lincolns of Massachusetts." Fish 1052.

375. WILLIAMS, ROBERT H. "GOD'S CHOSEN RULER." Frederick, Md., 1865. 8vo, three-quarter morocco. 500 copies. A.L.S. to Hart re book. Hart, Lambert copy. Fish 1055.

376. WILSON, RUFUS ROCKWELL. LINCOLN IN CARICATURE. *Illustrated with thirty-two plates.* Printed for private distribution, 1903. Folio, unbound, in half cloth, boards portfolio.

Limited to 150 copies, on Roxburgh Antique paper. Scarce. Fish 1062.

377. WOODBURY, AUGUSTUS. THE SON OF GOD CALLETH THE DEAD TO LIFE. A Sermon suggested by the Assassination of Abraham Lincoln. Providence, 1865. 12mo, three-quarter morocco. 300 copies printed. A.L.S. to Hart, referring to the pamphlet. Lambert copy. Fish 1067.

378. WOODBURY, AUGUSTUS. A SKETCH OF THE CHARACTER OF ABRAHAM LINCOLN. Providence, 1865. 12mo, three-quarter morocco. 300 copies. A.L.S. to Hart re book. Hart, Lambert copy. Fish 1068.

379. WORDS OF LINCOLN. THE PRESIDENT'S WORDS. [Edited by Edw. E. Hale] Boston, 1865. Original cloth. ✝ WORDS OF ABRAHAM

LINCOLN. Edited by C. W. French. New York (1894). Original wrappers, rebound in half cloth. Together two volumes, 16mo.

First edition of first mentioned. T.L.S. by E. E. Hale, 12mo, one page, Dec. 2, 1898, tipped in: "The Sunday after Lincoln's death, I made my sermon wholly from extracts of his writings . . . It was worked from the types for the immediate demand [4000 copies], and is now, I believe, quite a rare book." Fish 771 and 335.

380. **WORTMAN, DENIS.** A DISCOURSE ON THE DEATH OF PRESIDENT LINCOLN. Albany, 1865. 8vo, three-quarter morocco. 1000 copies. A.L.S. and envelope addressed to Hart re book. Lambert copy. Fish 1072.

MEDALS, NOS. 381 TO 391
ONE OF 5 COPIES

381. **MEDAL, THE LINCOLN CENTENNIAL.** THE LINCOLN CENTENNIAL MEDAL, Presenting the medal of Abraham Lincoln by Jules Edouard Roiné, Together with Papers on the Medal: Its Origin and Symbolism by **G. N.** Scott, etc. New York, 1908. 12mo, red morocco, gilt edges, with silver plate on front cover lettered: "The wood encasing the Medal in this book was part of the weather board on the house in Springfield, Illinois, occupied from 1844 to 1861 by Abraham Lincoln . . ." Back cover lettered: "Daniel H. Newhall from E. J. D."

Limited to 5 copies. Laid in is a letter from Mr. Newhall to Joseph McAleenan, explaining the history of the wood and the 5 medals. ‧ Tipped in is an affidavit testifying that the wood came from Lincoln's house, was cut for the bronze medal and delivered directly to Mr. Newhall.

382. **MEDAL, THE LINCOLN CENTENNIAL.** THE LINCOLN CENTENNIAL MEDAL. Presenting the Medal of Abraham Lincoln by Jules Edouard Roiné, etc. New York, 1908. 12mo, original cloth, gilt edges.

Unnumbered edition with bronze medal. Oakleaf 952.

383. **POLITICALS, FIRST CAMPAIGN.** King, No. 10. Obverse: "Abraham Lincoln. 1860." Reverse: Lincoln splitting rails, and streamer, lettered "Progress." 38mm., white metal. One of the earliest campaign medals.

384. **POLITICALS, FIRST CAMPAIGN.** King, No. 70. Obverse: Bust of Lincoln. Reverse: "Honest Abe of the West." 19mm., white metal. Claimed to be the first Politicals used.

385. **POLITICALS, FIRST CAMPAIGN.** King, Nos. 7, 12, 34. Bust Portraits of Lincoln, with various slogans on reverse: "Thou art the Man for President." "The People's Choice 1860, etc." "Let Liberty be National, etc." Together three medals 40mm., 38mm. and 31mm. respectively, white metal.

386. **POLITICALS, FIRST CAMPAIGN.** King Nos. 20, 42, 48, 58. Bust of Lincoln on obverse, with various slogans; "The Great Rail-Splitter of the West;" etc. Together four medals, 35mm., 27½mm., 27mm. and 22mm. respectively, brass.

387. POLITICALS, SECOND CAMPAIGN. King, Nos. 72, 75, 105, 110. Obverse sides: No. 72, portraits of Lincoln and Johnson with "War for the Union." 41½mm. No. 75, portrait of "Honest Old Abe." 34mm. No. 105, "Abraham Lincoln 1864." 22mm. No. 110, bust of Lincoln (Reverse, "Inaug. Second Term.") 18mm. Together four medals, white metal, last silver.

388. CIVIL WAR. King, No. 182. Obverse: Bust, encircled by "Abraham Lincoln President U. S. War of 1861." Reverse: blank with small circle. 29½mm., brass.

389. COMMEMORATIVES. King, No. 256. Obverse: Bust of Lincoln, facing left with slogan "Abrm. Lincoln The Martyr President." Reverse: circle of eagles and stars with inscription. 31mm., white metal. ✛King, No. 279. Obverse: oval bust of Lincoln, facing left. Reverse: pearled oval, with slogan "Martyr to Liberty." 24 x 21mm., copper. Together two medals.

390. EXPOSITION. King, No. 50. Obverse: bust of Lincoln, facing right, inscription "Memoria in Aeterna." Reverse: female figure, inscription "North-Western Sanitary Fair" and "Chicago, Ill." 1865. 57½mm., copper.

391. NUMISMATICS. The American Numismatic and Archæological Society. The Medallic History of Abraham Lincoln. By A. C. Zabriskie. New York, 1901. 4to. Fish 1079. ✛The Lincoln Centennial. The Robert Hewitt Collection of Medallic Lincolniana. 1909. 16mo. Oakleaf 1066. A.P.C. by Hewitt and invitation by Zabriskie. Together two pieces, wrappers.

PORTRAITS, PHOTOGRAPHS, ETC., NOS. 392 TO 439

392. ANONYMOUS. Two Original Water Colours. Lincoln as Flatboatman; and Lincoln as Rail-Splitter. Each 4″ x 5″, unframed.

393. ASSASSINATION. Broadside. "Our Martyr Presidents." Garfield and Lincoln. New York, Published by Charles Lubrecht, 1881. Coloured dramatic scenes of assassination of both presidents. 27″ x 36″, unframed.

394. BORGLUM, GUTZON. Wood Engraving. Head of Lincoln. *Engraved by Howard McCormick.* Signed by Borglum and McCormick, 1909. 9″ x 12″, framed.

395. [BOTELER, COL. A. R.] Two Caricature Drawings in Pen and Ink. "Where is Jackson?" (McClellan enquiring, Jackson behind a tree, about to attack.) "The Little Napoleon Receives another Pointed Reminder." (Lincoln prodding McClellan with a pitchfork. 1862.) 5″ x 3″ and 5″ x 5″, mounted on one sheet. Endorsed at bottom as "Southern caricatures owned by Col. Strother in 1874." Two A.L.S. by Strother and A.L.S. by Pierre Morand. Latter re drawings, saying at least one was done by Col. A. R. Boteler of Gen. Lee's staff.

AUTOGRAPHED BY LINCOLN

396. BRADY, MATHEW. ORIGINAL PHOTOGRAPH SIGNED BY LINCOLN. 3½" x 2¾6". Represents Lincoln seated beside a table, holding his spectacles in one hand and a sheet of paper in the other.
The negative was taken by Mathew Brady in Washington, early in 1863, soon after the first Emancipation Proclamation. Meserve No. 53. A.L.S. by John Hay, Oct. 8, 1864: "... the President desires me to transmit three copies of his photograph and autograph for the 'Illinois Street Union Sabbath Schools.' of Chicago ..." Letter and photograph laid in "Portrait Life of Lincoln" by F. T. Miller. Oakleaf 985.

397. BROADSIDE. LINCOLN AND HIS GENERALS, in Colour. New York, Published by Ensign & Bridgeman, no date. 28" x 34", unframed.

398. BUTTRE, J. C. ENGRAVED PORTRAIT. Bust of Lincoln. N. Y., Engraved and published by J. C. Buttre [1865]. Oval 7½" x 10", with border designs by Momberger.

399. CHROMO-LITHOGRAPH. BUST PORTRAIT OF LINCOLN, facing right. Oval, 13" x 16", framed.

400. CHROMO-LITHOGRAPH. ABRAHAM LINCOLN. Bust portrait, attractively coloured. 13" x 16", framed.

401. COLOURED ENGRAVING. A Council of War in 1861, at the President's House. Seated around the table are Lincoln, Seward, Scott, Cameron, McClellan, Butler, Wool, Anderson, Fremont and Dix. New York, Geo. E. Perine, 1866. 16" x 12", unframed.

402. CONFEDERATE WAR ETCHINGS. Twenty-nine etchings with index. The first three include Lincoln. Printed on thin paper, mounted on cardboard.

ONE OF THREE COPIES RECORDED

403. CURRIER AND IVES. LITHOGRAPH. "Hon. Abraham Lincoln. Republican Candidate for Sixteenth President of the United States." From a Photograph by Brady, beardless bust, facing right. N. Y., Currier & Ives, 1860. Large folio, framed. Peters, No. 1870.
The addition of the beard, late in 1860, makes this first issue very rare and highly desirable.

404. CURRIER AND IVES. LITHOGRAPH CARTOON. "Progressive Democracy—Prospect of a Smash Up." New York, Currier and Ives, 1860. 17" x 13", unframed.
The very interesting grade crossing cartoon, showing the Lincoln and Hamlin engine about to crash into the Democratic wagon, to opposite ends of which are hitched Douglas and Johnson and Breckenridge and Lane. Peters 1672.

405. CURRIER AND IVES. COLOURED LITHOGRAPH. "The Lincoln Family." N. Y., Currier and Ives, 1867. 14" x 11¾", unframed.

406. CURRIER AND IVES. LITHOGRAPH. "The Nation's Martyr." (Light foxing) ✚ COLOURED LITHOGRAPH. "Mrs. Lincoln." Each 9" x 13", unframed.

[51]

407. DAGUERREOTYPES. Two Tintype Portraits of Lincoln. One Cooper Union portrait and an early portrait with folded arms. In daguerreotype cases for protection.

408. GASPARD. Original Charcoal Sketch Signed. Head portrait of Lincoln, front view. 13" x 19", framed.

409. HAMBRIDGE, JAY. Three Original Drawings Signed, in Charcoal and Pencil. Illustrations to "He Knew Lincoln," by Ida M. Tarbell. Three scenes, each 12" x 18" on tinted paper, framed together. Lambert collection.

410. HAMBRIDGE, JAY. Two Original Drawings Signed, in Charcoal and Pencil. Illustrations to "He Knew Lincoln," by Ida M. Tarbell. Each 9" x 12", framed together. Lambert collection.

411. HESSLER. The Ayres' reprint of the Hessler 1860 portrait. 6" x 8½", framed. Vide A.L.S. re portrait,. No. 477.

412. HOLLIS, L. Original Wash Drawing. "Abraham Lincoln Entering Richmond, April 3rd, 1865." 18" x 13", unframed. ✚Steel Engraving. Same scene. By J. C. Buttre, 1866. Together two pieces.

413. HUNT, ALBERT. Original Pencil Drawing Signed. Lincoln seated in a store, resting his head on his right hand and leaning on a table. Signed: "Albert Hunt. City Point, Va. March 27th, 1865." 6" x 9", framed.

414. LINCOLN, ABRAHAM. Lithograph. "Proclamation of Emancipation." With small portrait of Lincoln in centre. *Designed and executed by A. Kidder.* Lithographed by Chas. Shober, Chicago, 1862. 18" x 22", unframed; some damp-staining and partly strengthened back.

ONLY THREE COPIES KNOWN

415. LINCOLN, ABRAHAM. Facsimile of the Emancipation Proclamation, and the Letter to the Ladies in Charge of the North-Western Fair. Chicago, Published and lithographed by Ed. Mendel, 1863. 24" x 29", unframed; somewhat cracked and mounted on fabric. Small photograph of Lincoln, by Wenderoth and Taylor pasted on.

POSSIBLY UNIQUE

416. LITHOGRAPH. First Campaign Lithograph Portrait. Tinted bust portrait, facing right. Chicago, Lithographed and published by Ed. Mendel, [1860]. 13" x 15", in split-rail frame. Rare, if not unique.

417. LITHOGRAPH. Bust Portrait, facing right. Chicago, Kurz & Allison, no date. 22" x 27", framed.

418. LITHOGRAPH. Abraham Lincoln, Bust in wreath. N. Y., Kellogg, Hartford, and Whiting. Published by Colden and Sammons, Chicago. Oval, 9" x 12", walnut frame.

419. LITHOGRAPH. Abraham Lincoln. N. Y., Published by Kimmel & Forster. Oval, 6″ x 8″, tinted, in antique rectangular frame.

420. [LITTLEFIELD] Engraved Bust Portrait. 22″ x 28″, framed. Fine copy of this important portrait, by Littlefield.

421. LLOYD. Lloyd's New Political Chart [in colour]. Portrait of Lincoln, centre, with group portraits of his cabinet below, and of Generals Scott, Butler, Ellsworth and Anderson in corners. Also Map of U. S. showing area of seceded states. N. Y., H. H. Lloyds, 1861. 30″ x 36″, wall chart with rules top and bottom for hanging.

422. McRAE, JOHN C. Engraved Portrait. Abraham Lincoln. N. Y., Engraved and published by John C. McRae [1865]. Oval, 9″ x 11″, with border designs.

423. [MORAND, PIERRE] Original Pencil Drawing. Lincoln seated in a store, similar to the Hunt drawing. "City Point, Va., 27 March 1865." 4″ x 6″, unframed. A.L.S. by Morand laid in re drawing and connection with Hunt.

424. NAST, THOMAS. Original Drawing Signed. Combination Pen and Ink and Wash. Reproduced in Harper's Weekly, 1865. Four portraits, upper centre, of Washington, Grant, Lee and Lincoln, each wreathed with his best-known saying. Below is a rural scene, a soldier back at the plow, with wife and children, quoting Grant to Lee: "Tell your men to take their horses home with them to help them make their crops." Unquestionably one of Nast's masterpieces. 15″ x 21″, unframed.

425. NAST, THOMAS. Original Pen and Ink Sketch Signed. Cemetery scene with inscription on headstone: "Warning to Workingmen," quoted from Lincoln's message to Congress. Spirit of Lincoln sketched in, pointing to his address. Signed: "Th. Nast, 1888." 14″ x 22″, framed.

426. PEARSON, RALPH M. Original Etching Signed. "Lincoln's Birthplace." January 1915. 5″ x 7″, unframed.

EXCEEDINGLY RARE

427. PHOTOGRAPH. Original Photograph. The Chicago Delegation that accompanied Lincoln's Body to Springfield; taken in front of Lincoln's home. 15″ x 12″, old walnut frame. Among those present were, N. K. Fairbank, J. B. Bradwell, B. W. Raymond, I. L. Milliken, J. H. Woodworth, M. Talcott, G. S. Hubbard, M. Skinner, G. P. A. Healey, J. H. McVicker, Dr. D. Brainard, J. H. Kinzie, and 93 others.

428. PHOTOGRAPH. "Abraham Lincoln at Home." Philadelphia, Published by Charles Desilver, 1865. Lincoln's Springfield home with Lincoln seated on the front veranda. 8″ x 6″. With Lincoln's Farewell Address to his old neighbors beneath.

429. PHOTOGRAPH. Profile Portrait, facing right. Copy of a Photograph. Oval, 5″ x 7″, framed.

430. PHOTOGRAPHS. Four photographs of Lincoln. Two carte-de-visite portraits, one of Lincoln's head and one of him seated with his family. Two photographic copies, one the Cooper Union portrait· and one head, presented to Mrs. Lucy **G**. Speed.

431. PHOTOGRAPHS. A Collection of forty-one Cabinet Photographs, each autographed by the person represented.
An interesting collection, including C. A. Bartol, G. S. Boutwell, H. Butterworth, J. H. Choate, E. E. Hale, J. F. Clarke, W. D. Howells, C. E. Norton, Whitelaw Reid, A. K. McClure, etc.

432. PORTRAITS. A Collection of nineteen Prints, comprising thirteen Steel Engravings and others. Head portraits of Lincoln. One half-tone cut of Hessler, 1860. A.L.S. of A. S. Edwards, Custodian of the Lincoln Home, and nephew of Lincoln.

433. PORTRAIT CATALOGUES. A Catalogue of a Collection of Engraved and Other Portraits of Lincoln. New York, The Grolier Club, 1899. 12mo. Fish 365. ✚Catalogue of the Portraits of Lincoln. Plainfield, N. J., Judd Stewart, [1912]. Oakleaf 1119. 8vo. Together two pamphlets, wrappers.

434. SARTAIN, WILLIAM. Engraved portraits. "Abraham Lincoln," and "Mrs. Lincoln." N. Y., Engraved and published by William Sartain. 9″ x 11″, unframed.

435. SCHNEIDER, OTTO. Original Etching Signed. Head of Lincoln in 1858. 8″ x 11½″, unframed.

436. SMITH, WILLIAM. Lithograph. Bust portrait. Philadelphia, published by William Smith, no date. 21″ x 27″, unframed.

437. STRONG, THOMAS W. Lithograph Cartoon. "Our National Bird as it Appeared when Handed to James Buchanan. March 4, 1857. The Identical Bird as it Appeared A.D. 1861." New York, 1861. 14″ x 11″, unframed.
Very rare cartoon showing the American Eagle crippled by Anarchy and Secession, saying: "'I was murdered i' the Capitol' Shakespeare."

438. STROTHER, D. H. [Porte Crayon] Two Original Drawings Signed, in Water colour. First represents Lincoln in blue frock coat and top hat, full length, standing. 4″ x 7″. Signed: "D.H.S. at Richmond, 1865." Second India ink drawing tinted, full length in street dress. 3″ x 6″. Signed: "D.H.S., 1864." The two framed together.

439. VOLK, DOUGLAS. Original Pen and Ink Sketch Signed. Lincoln's Life Mask. Inscribed: "From the original cast taken from the face of A. Lincoln by Leonard Volk—Drawn by Douglas Volk." 7″ x 10″, unframed.

440. ANDERSON, ROBERT. Commander, Fort Sumter. A.L.S. 4to, 1p. Augusta, Maine, March 26, 1839. To his mother.
Fine letter, discussing the boundary fight of Maine, and mentioning Genl. Scott.

441. ASHMAN, GEORGE. Chairman of Chicago 1860 Convention. Two A.L.S. 4to, 2pp. (1856) and 3pp. (no year). Anticipates going to Washington. Also engraved portrait.

442. ASSASSINATION. A.L.S. by Julia A. Shepherd. 8vo, 8pp. Hopeton, April 16, 1865. To her father.
A remarkable letter from a young lady who attended Ford's Theatre the evening of the assassination. She describes the entire situation and all events in careful detail.

443. BANCROFT, GEORGE. Historian. T.L.S. 4to, 1p. Newport, R. I. July 25, 1887. To J. G. Wilson, congratulating him on his book. ✚D.S. 4to, 2pp. 1846. From the Navy Department.

444. BATES, EDWARD. Lincoln's Attorney-General. A.L.S. 8vo, 2pp. Washington, Nov. 13, 1864. To James E. Yeatman, St. Louis. Marked "Private," refers to Lincoln.

445. [BOURNE, EDWARD E.] Historian of Kennebunk, Me. ORIGINAL A. MS. "Eulogy of Abraham Lincoln." 4to, 34pp. [Kennebunk, Me., 1865] Not in Fish or Oakleaf. Burton sale, 180.

446. BRAGG, GEN. BRAXTON. Confederate general. A.L.S. 8vo, 4pp. April 13, 1861. To his wife. ✚A.L.S. by Col. D. Urquhart. 8vo, 4pp. Richmond, July 6, 1865. To Gen. Bragg. Together two pieces.
Superb letter of Bragg to his wife, reading, in part: "Well, the war has commenced, and a long and bloody one it will be unless our people go into it with spirit and make Mr. Lincoln feel it at once. Washington City ought to be seized, and Scott and Lincoln brought South." Col. Urquhart's letter mentions Jefferson Davis, Lee and Grant.

447. BROWNLOW, W. G. Tennessee minister. Two A.L.S. 8vo, 1p. each. Washington, 1862; and Cincinnati, 1863. Second mentioned to H. C. Whitney, requesting his pay for service as Army chaplain. ✚A.D.S. by Whitney on verso of Brownlow's letter, endorsing the request.

448. BUCHANAN, JAMES. Fifteenth President of U. S. D.S. Consular appointment. Folio, parchment. Jan. 18, 1855. Also a cut signature.

449. CABINET. LINCOLN AND HIS CABINET. A Collection of Autographs. 1861-1865. Folio, full blue levant morocco, deep gilt ruled borders, dentelles and tops, moiré silk doublures.
Inlaid autograph material and engraved portraits. Abraham Lincoln, D.S., consular approval, signed in full, Sept. 24, 1864. Then follow A.L.S. and L.S. of Hamlin, Seward, Chase, Cameron, Stanton, Welles, Bates, Speed, McCulloch, Dennison, Fessenden.

450. CAMERON, SIMON. Lincoln's Secretary of War. Four A.N.S. 1853-1870. One states he was appointed secretary March 4, 1861 and resigned Jan. 12, 1862. With two cut signatures.

451. [CHANDLER, CAPT. (?)] Original A. MS. Description of the Use of Torpedoes in the Civil War. Folio, 6pp. With A.N.S. by Benj. Lessing, telling how Chandler cleared a torpedo mined canal for Lincoln's proceeding.

452. CHASE, SALMON P. Lincoln's First Secretary of the Treasury. Two A.L.S. 4to, 3pp., Washington, 1829 and 8vo, 1p., Columbus, 1860. Also D.S. and cut signature.

453. CIVIL WAR GENERALS. A Collection of twenty-eight A.L.S. and cut signatures, with four engravings. Includes Sherman, Thomas, Burnside, Hancock, Butler, Wheeler, Buell, Hooker, Pope, Logan, Meade, McClellan, etc.

454. CLAY, HENRY. American statesman. Two A.L.S. 4to and 8vo, 1p. each. Ashland, 21st July, 1842; Washington 27th Feb. 1851, with original envelope.

First mentioned a fine letter to Dr. I. Hendershott saying, in part: "You do me the favor to express your regrets that I was not nominated by the Philad. Convention as the Whig Candidate for the Presidency. Ought you not rather to congratulate me on the event? I believe that I should have been elected with ease, if I had been nominated; . . ."

455. COLLINS, RICHARD H. A. MS.S. The Lincolns and Old Salem. 8vo, 4pp. La Parier, Courier Journal, 1886. With typescript copy.

456. CONFEDERATE TELEGRAMS. A Collection of five from Lee, Breckenridge and Forrest; one dated April 10, 1865, one of the last acts of the Confederacy. Also broadside printed orders of Bragg at Chattanooga, Aug. 25, 1862.

457. DANA, C. A. Editor of The New York Sun. Four A.L.S. 8vo, 2pp. each. New York, 1868, '79, '95, '96.

458. DAVIS, JEFFERSON. President of the Confederacy. A.L.S. 8vo, 1p. No date. ✚D.S. Washington, 1853. ✚Cut signature. Together three pieces.

459. DOUGLAS, STEPHEN A. A Collection of Newspaper clippings, two engraved portraits, A.N.S., A.L.S. (4to, 1p. Chicago, Oct. 5, 1849) and Breckenridge and Lane Campaign Documents, No. 9. Reply of J. Davis to the Speech of Sen. Douglas, 1860.

A fine letter marked "Private," relating to railroads, saying that Council Bluffs was the true starting place for all lines East.

460. EDITORS. A Collection of eight A.L.S. by Thurlow Weed, Noah Brooks, Frank G. Carpenter, Whitelaw Reid, W. S. Thayer and Henry J. Raymond.

461. EVERETT, EDWARD. Orator and statesman. A. MS. S. Copy of his Gettysburg Address. 4to, 3pp. Boston, Jan. 18, 1864. With a fine engraved portrait of Everett by Sartain.

462. EVERETT, EDWARD. Two A.L.S. 4to, 1p. and 4pp. Council Chamber, Jan. 7, 1839 and Boston, Dec. 11, 1845. Also cut signature. Mentions literary and political affairs.

463. FELL, JESSE W. STORY OF THE LINCOLN AUTOBIOGRAPHY. [Bloomington, March, 1872] 8vo, 2 leaves, printed on one side. ✦A.L.S. by Mrs. Charles Sabin Taft and two others.

464. FESSENDEN, WILLIAM. Maine Republican senator. SIX A.L.S. 1856-1868. On various public questions.

465. FORD, JOHN T. Proprietor of Ford's Theatre. A.L.S. 4to, 1p. Baltimore, June 12, 1859. Fine dramatic letter re suitable plays. Written on verso of A.L.S. by Lilly Dawson, actress-manager, re productions.

466. GALLAGHER, W. D. ORIGINAL A. POEM S. "The President's Gun." 4to, 4pp. January 27, 1863. 3 verses of 8 lines each.
Begins: "Ratify! ratify!—Ratify what?.
The President's Proclamation!"

467. GENERALS. ABRAHAM LINCOLN AND HIS GENERALS. A Collection of Autographs. 1861-1865. Folio, full blue levant morocco, deep gilt ruled borders, dentelles and tops, moiré silk doublures.
Inlaid autograph material and engraved portraits. Abraham Lincoln, 3 line autograph endorsement, Sept. 1, 1864, on envelope regarding military matters. Grant D.S.; Sherman, 3pp. A.L.S.; also A.L.S. and L.S. of the following: Sheridan, Thomas, Scott, McClellan, Burnside, Hooker, Halleck, Hancock, Fremont, Butler, Dix, Schofield, Wool, Logan, Pope, Porter, Sickles, Newton, Kilpatrick.

UNPUBLISHED MANUSCRIPT NOTES

468. GURLEY, P. D. Lincoln's minister in Washington. A Collection of MANUSCRIPT NOTES written by Dr. Gurley who evidently intended to write an intimate Private Life of Lincoln in Washington. Each written on note paper of the period and relating some Saying or Anecdote of Lincoln. With the name of each story endorsed on verso: "Little Tad's Tooth Extracted;" "John Brown's Spear;" "Tells Seward how to tell a Story;" "Lincoln's Homeliness;" "Preparations for Flight;" "Story of the Pigs;" "Society Belle and Mr. Lincoln;" "Moses;" "Speeches to the Soldiers;" "Style of Dress;" "Independence of Mr. Lincoln;" etc. 57 pieces. With affidavit. 1861-5. ALL UNPUBLISHED.

469. HALE, EDWARD E. American author. Two A.L.S. 1889, 1904. Two signatures. Together four pieces.

470. HAMLIN, HANNIBAL. Lincoln's Vice-president. A Collection of six A.L.S. (1860-1890), three signatures and an autographed photograph.

471. HANKS, DENNIS F. Lincoln's maternal uncle. A.L.S. Oblong 4to, 1p., framed. Charleston, Illinois, March 21, 1870. To Andrew Boyd. Retraced in 1908 for faded ink, and framed.

Writes about a watch chain he had which Lincoln had owned for 20 years, making a drawing of same; also saying where Mr. Boyd could obtain some of the rails of the Lincoln cabin. Hanks, at the Chicago Convention, entered the Wigwam with one of the celebrated rails split by Lincoln, and started the furore which resulted in his nomination. Burton sale, 389.

472. HAY, JOHN. Lincoln's secretary. A.N.S. (1899); T.N.S. (1901); and one signature.

473. HERNDON, WILLIAM H. Lincoln's law partner. AUTO-GRAPH RECORD BOOK SIGNED. "Corporations Private." Square 8vo, original calf; rubbed.

A. L. S. by H. E. Barker, dealer in Lincolniana laid in; May 16, 1916, 8vo, one page "Abraham Lincoln's law partner for twenty years, Wm. Herndon, opened up this little 'Records' book . . . and it was turned over to Gen'l Alfred Orendorff, his law partner from 1873 to 1877, when Herndon retired from active practise in 1877. Quite a number of books used by Lincoln and Herndon were thus acquired by Mr. Orendorff, and were afterwards purchased by me from the family, this vol. being among the number."

474. HERNDON, WILLIAM H. A.L.S. 4to, 4 full pages. Springfield, Ills., Feb. 18th, 1886. To "Friend Fonlen." Broken at centre fold, text unimpaired.

Magnificent letter on the fatalism of Lincoln: " . . . Mr. Lincoln believed that what was to be would be and no prayers of ours could arrest or reverse the decree . . . that the conditions made the man—does make the man . . . that general-universal and eternal laws governed both matter and mind . . . His calmness under bloody war was the result . . . Emmerson had the genius of the spiritual and ideal. Lincoln had the genius of the real and the practical. Emmerson lived high among the stars. Lincoln lived low among men. Emmerson dreamed, Lincoln acted. Emmerson was intuitional, Lincoln reflective . . . Both were liberals in religion and were great men."

475. HERNDON, WILLIAM H. A.L.S. 4to, 2pp., closely written. Springfield, Ills., Sept. 10, 1887. To "Friend Remsberg." ✦BRIEF ANALYSIS OF LINCOLN'S CHARACTER. A Letter to J. E. Remsberg from William H. Herndon. Privately printed, 1917. 8vo, 4 leaves. Limited to 50 copies, signed by Barker. Oakleaf 621. ✦A.L.S. by Barker 8vo, 1p. To Little, re Herndon's letter.

The original letter by Herndon and the pamphlet printed from it. Unusual comment on Lincoln's character and Speed's influence on him. In part: "Probably, except in his love scrapes, Lincoln never poured out his soul to any mortal creature at anytime and on no subject. He was the most secretive—reticent—shut-mouthed man that ever existed. You had to guess at the man after years of acquaintance . . . he loved principle, but moved ever just to suit his own ends; he was a trimmer among men . . . they were his tools and instruments; he was a cool man—an unsocial one—an abstracted one . . ."

476. HERNDON, WILLIAM H. A. MS. S. "Mrs. Lincoln's Denial and What SHE Says." Springfield, Ills., Jan. 12th 1874. 12mo. 22 pages; in three-quarter morocco book. MSS. attributed to Herndon, on an interview with Mrs. Lincoln and the notes he took from her for his book.

477. HESSLER PHOTOGRAPH. Two A.L.S. to Mr. Ayres, regarding the Ayres reprint of the Hessler photograph.

John T. Hanks (Colvig amanuensis), 4to, 1p. June 4, 1902: "I unhesitatingly pronounce it the most lifelike and realistic picture of him I have ever seen." Jesse W. Weik, 4to, 2pp. Feb. 20, 1893. In part: "[Herndon] regarded it as the most literal and characteristic portrait of all. 'He's a little fixed up,' he said, referring to the unusual neatness of dress, 'but there is the peculiar curve of the lower lip, the lone mole on the right cheek and a pose of the head so essentially Lincolnian no other artist has ever caught it.'"

478. JOHNSON, ANDREW. Seventeenth President of U. S. D.S. Senate nomination. Folio, 1p. Executive Mansion; July 18, 1868.

479. JUSSERAND, JULES. French Ambassador to the U. S. ORIGINAL A. MS. S. "Brandywine Commemoration, Sept. 11, 1919 (sic)." 4to, 3pp. With T.L.S. Washington, Sept. 30, 1915.

480. LIEBER, FRANCIS. Scientist. A.L.S. 4to, 4pp. New York, Oct. 14, 1868. Re the significance of "e pluribus unum." ✛A.L.S. 8vo, 3pp., mounted. N. Y. 1870. Re the enlisting of slaves in the war.

481. LINCOLN, ABRAHAM. A.D.S. "Logan & Lincoln." Court order. Horatio M. Vandeveer vs. James Baker, regarding school lands. Folio, 1p. Circa 50 words and endorsement in Lincoln's hand. Filed 1844.

482. LINCOLN, ABRAHAM. A.D.S. "Logan & Lincoln." Legal Document: "The Replication of Nathaniel Hay to the answer of Nicholas Bryan, etc." Folio, 1p., 13 lines and endorsement in Lincoln's hand. Filed May, 1847.

483. LINCOLN, ABRAHAM. A.L.S. 4to, 1p. Washington, Feb. 4, 1848. To "Friend M'Callen."

Refers to the Mexican war: "There is now some possibility of peace; but should the war go on, I think volunteers, with the right of electing their own officers will be voted, but that no more regulars will be voted—Until Congress shall act, of course, nothing can be done towards getting your regiment into service—Whenever it shall act I shall be happy to assist you in any way I can. Yours truly A. Lincoln. P. S. Don't pay postage on letters to me—I am entitled to them free. A. L."

484. [LINCOLN, ABRAHAM] LEGAL DOCUMENT. Cross bill in Chancery, Vermillion County. Folio, 2pp. Oct. 22, 1850. Circa 50 lines in Lincoln's hand. John Van Gundy vs. Joseph Gundy.

485. LINCOLN, ABRAHAM. LEGAL DOCUMENT SIGNED (twice). "Davis, Lincoln & Lamon." Folio, 1p. June 2, 1853. Circa 20 lines in Lincoln's hand. Endorsed on verso with large "L." "William Bachop ads. William M. Samm."

486. LINCOLN, ABRAHAM. LEGAL DOCUMENT SIGNED. "Lincoln & Lamon." 8vo, 1p. May 30, 1854. Circa 10 lines in Lincoln's hand. "Joseph B. Lamon ads. Samuel Titus & George W. Titus, In Assumpsit."

487. [LINCOLN, ABRAHAM] LEGAL DOCUMENT. Mortgage between Peter R. Leonard and John Villars. Folio, 2pp. May 26, 1854.
Circa 60 lines in Lincoln's hand.

488. LINCOLN, ABRAHAM. A.L.S. 4to, 1p. Springfield, Sept.
7, 1854. To A. B. Moreau.

*Characteristic campaign letter: "Stranger tho, I am, personally, being a brother in
the faith, I venture to write you. Yates cannot come to your court next week . . .
Hains will be with you, head up and tail up, for Nebraska—You must have some-
one to make an Anti-Nebraska speech—Palmer is the best . . . Jo. Gillespie, if
you cannot get Palmer—and somebody anyhow . . . Yours etc. A. Lincoln."*

489. LINCOLN, ABRAHAM. LEGAL DOCUMENT SIGNED (twice).
Folio, 1p. [Springfield, 1859] Legal plea and Notice; "Michael
Courtney ads. Erastus Fortune." Circa 24 lines in Lincoln's hand.

JUSTICE AND FAIRNESS TO ALL

490. LINCOLN, ABRAHAM. A.L.S. 12mo, 1p. Springfield, Ills.,
Aug. 14, 1860. To T. A. Cheney.

*"I would cheerfully answer your questions in regard to the Fugitive Slave law,
were it not that I consider it would be both imprudent, and contrary to the reason-
able expectation of friends, for me to write, or speak anything upon doctrinal points
now—Besides this, my published speeches contain nearly all I could willingly say—
Justice, and fairness to all, is the utmost I have said, or will say.—Yours truly A.
Lincoln."*

491. LINCOLN, ABRAHAM. A.L.S. 8vo, 1p. Executive Mansion, April 10, 1861. To the Hon. Sec. of Treasury. Facsimile laid in.

*"Mr. Wood thinks that possibly he can save you something in the matter of en-
graving Treasury Notes—Please give him an interview, & see what there is of it.
Yours truly A. Lincoln."*

492. LINCOLN, ABRAHAM. D.S. Consular approval. Folio, 1p.,
parchment. Washington, Sept. 18, 1862. Countersigned by William H.
Seward.

*Signed on the day of the battle of Antietam-Chartsburg, that ended in a victory
for the North. Lincoln, began to write the Emancipation Proclamation on this
day.*

493. LINCOLN, ABRAHAM. D.S. Commission. Folio, 1p. vellum.
Washington, March 17, 1863. Countersigned by Edwin M. Stanton.

494. [LINCOLN, ABRAHAM] AUTOGRAPH ENDORSEMENT. Verso
of folio, 2pp. April 7, 1863. "Memorial & Petition on Judgeship of
N. C. W. H. Doherty, Newburn, N. C."

495. LINCOLN, ABRAHAM. D.S. Pardon for Joseph Shoemaker.
4to, 1p. Washington, April 20, 1863. Signed in full.

496. LINCOLN, ABRAHAM. A.N.S. Card mounted. June 11,
1863.

*"Col. R. W. Thompson is my friend, whom I would be glad to have obliged in any
way not inconsistent with the public interest. A. Lincoln." Fine association item
with the author of "Personal Recollections. Washington to Lincoln."*

497. LINCOLN, **ABRAHAM.** D.S. IN FULL. Pardon of George Hamilton. 4to, 1p. Feb. 23, 1864.

498. LINCOLN, **ABRAHAM.** D.S. Consular appointment signed in full. Folio, 1p. June 13, 1864. Countersigned by William H. Seward.

499. LINCOLN, **ABRAHAM.** A.D.S. "Lincoln and Herndon." Oblong 16mo, 1p. Legal plea, 5 lines.

500. [LINCOLN, **ABRAHAM**] ENVELOPE ADDRESSED. "Hon. Attorney General Present. From the President."

501. (LINCOLN) LINCOLN SCRAP BOOK. 4to, three-quarter roan; worn.
This album was formerly the property of Dr. J. B. English (with autograph), a personal friend of Lincoln. A. Index S. by J. E. Burton lists; six signatures of Lincoln; old style pictures of Lincoln and friends; Gettysburg speech, in mourning border with engraved portrait; Lincoln stamp envelope (scarce); A.L.S., 2pp., of Union soldier; photo of old mint at New Orleans; picture of J. W. Booth; hanging the four conspirators; etc.

502. (LINCOLN) Two Letters on the Origin of the Term, "Honest Abe." A.L.S. by R. W. Thompson. 4to, 2pp. Terre Haute, Dec. 1, 1894. ✠T.L.S. by Cullom. 4to, 2pp. Washington, D. C. Dec. 11, 1894.
Mr. Cullom claims that: "The first time I heard Mr. Lincoln called 'Honest Abe' was in the State Convention of Illinois in 1860." Mr. Thompson says: " . . . It was given him before he was elected to Congress or became President, . . . it must have originated with the people of Illinois, among whom he was looked upon as a plain and unostentatious man, and who affixed this title to his name in consequence of the simplicity of his conduct and plainness of dress and manner."

503. (LINCOLN) Two testimonials from citizens of Iowa, recommending appointments. Containing autographs of S. F. Smith, J. W. Rankin, J. W. Thompson, etc.

504. LINCOLN, **MRS. ABRAHAM.** A.L.S. 8vo, 1p. Executive Mansion, Feb. 26, 1864. To Messrs. Clement, Heerdt & Co., N. Y.
Copy for a telegram: "A telegram was sent you in reference to a basket of champaign. Please send a basket of the kind requested, also another one, of the choicest quality you have in store. Mrs. Lincoln." Broken at fold, bottom torn off, text unimpaired.

505. LINCOLN, **MRS. ABRAHAM.** A.L.S. 8vo, 1p. Dec. 24th, [1864]. Carte-de-visite photograph laid in.
Interesting letter to W. P. Fessenden, Sect'y of the Treasury: "Sir, The President has fully endorsed the recommendation of Mr. G. Gumpert for the appointment as collector or purchasing agent for Pensacola . . . You would oblige me very much by giving this appointment . . . I would like to know what prospects he has . . . Resp. Mrs. L."

506. LINCOLN, **ROBERT TODD.** Lincoln's son. A Collection of an A.L.S. (1880); T.L.S. (1887); two D.S. (1884); and three cut signatures.

507. LITERARY AUTOGRAPHS. A Collection of fourteen A.L.S. by I. Bachellor, J. Benton, R. Blanchard, **G**. H. Boker, M. A. Livermore, W. **D**. Howells, A. **K**. McClure, J. W. Howe, J. R. **G**ilmore, E. Eggleston, **G**. T. Curtis and E. S. Brooks. Also some original envelopes and cut signatures.

508. McCULLOCH, HUGH. Lincoln's Secretary of the Treasury. A.L.S., 1865 re character of Mr. Conness; Autographed photograph; two D.S., Treasury Dept. stationery; one signature.

509. MARKENS, ISAAC. Lincoln collector. Two A.L.S. 4to, 1p. Jan. 23, 1908. And 4to, 2pp. Jan. 25, 1908. To Major Lambert. *Fine long letter discussing detailed differences in the various issues of the Ford Theatre playbills on the night of the assassination.*

510. MASTERS, EDGAR LEE. American poet. A. POEM S. Last 7 lines of "Ann Rutledge" from "Spoon River Anthology." 12mo, 1p. March 8th, 1916.
"I am Ann Rutledge
Who lie beneath these weeds
Beloved in life of Abraham Lincoln
Wedded to him not through union
But through separation.
Bloom forever, O Republic,
From the dust of my bosom!"

511. NEALY, MARY E. A. MS. POEM S. "Veritas Vincit." Folio, 2pp. Washington, D. C., no date. 4 stanzas of 8 lines each. "Written after the death of Lincoln."

512. NEELY, WINFIELD SCOTT. A. MS. S. "Reminiscences of Eighteen Months Sojourn in Confederate Prisons." Folio, 88pp.; edges frayed. Highly interesting and presumably unpublished manuscript.

513. SERMON. A. MS. Sermon on the Death of Lincoln. By a prominent clergyman. 4to, 8pp. From the famous **G**. H. Moore collection.

514. SEWARD, WILLIAM H. Lincoln's Secretary of State. A.L.S. 4to, 1p. Dec. 22, 1843. On author's copyright. ✚A.L.S. 8vo, 1p. Nov. 8, 1852. Predicting: . . . that the Whig party will cease to be after Nov. 2. ✚D.S. 4to, 1p. 1865. ✚ENVELOPE S. Together four pieces.

515. SHIELDS, GEN. JAMES. 'Duellist.' THREE A.L.S. Two 4to, 1p. and one 8vo, 3pp. Washington, 1850, 1853 and 1878. Also cut signature, two engraved portraits and clippings.

516. SMITH, GREEN CLAY. ORIGINAL A. MS. S. "Lincoln and the Rebel's Boots." 4to, 4pp. Frankfort, **Ky**. Also printed copy laid in.

517. SMITH, S. FRANCIS. American poet. A. MS. S. "My Country 'Tis of Thee." 4to, 1p. 4 stanzas of 7 lines each. ✚A.L.S. 8vo, 1p. 1889. In reply to an autograph seeker.

518. STEPHENS, ALEXANDER H. Vice-president of Confederacy. A.L.S. 8vo, 4pp. Crawfordville, Ga., June 10, 1871. To Hon. James Burke (?). With autographed card. Fine long letter on usurpation of powers by Congress in reconstruction measures.

519. STOWE, HARRIET B. American novelist. A.L.S. 8vo, 4pp. No place or date. To Rev. Henry F. Allen. Fine personal letter. Also cut signature.

THE ORIGINAL OFFICIAL MS. REPORT OF LINCOLN'S ASSASSINATION, DEATH AND AUTOPSY

520. TAFT, DR. CHARLES SABIN. ORIGINAL A. MS. S. "Abraham Lincoln's Last Hours, The Note Book of an Army Surgeon present at the Assassination, Death and Autopsy." 4to, 16pp. With typescript and affidavit, signed by Taft's son, authenticating the MS. and copy.

The account begins: "The notes from which this article is written were made the day succeeding Mr. Lincoln's death, and immediately after the official examination of the body. They were made by direction of Secretary Stanton for the purpose of preserving an official account of the circumstances attending the assassination, in connection with the medical aspects of the case." Dr. Sabin describes the assassination in detail, having been an eye witness.

521. TARBELL, IDA M. Lincoln's biographer. Two T. MS. S. ["Introduction to Tracy's Collected Letters"] 4to, 6pp. "Memo of Talk with Gilbert Tracy, April 4, 1916." 4to, 4pp. ✚T.L.S. 4to, 1p. New York, Dec. 10, 1917. To Frank Bruce. Together three pieces.

Interesting collection of related material, inscribed for Mr. Little. Reads, in part: "I have the memo of my first talk with Mr. Tracy and my impressions of the first reading of [the] letters . . . From this memo I finally dictated the introduction, practically as it stands."

522. THOMPSON, MAURICE. American poet. Two A. MS. S. "To the South." 8vo, 4pp. Verse on Freedom. 8vo, 1p., 9 lines. ✚Two A.L.S. 16mo, 2pp. 1891. And 8vo, 3pp. 1892. News clippings and prints laid in.

Superb poem on the South, written with intense feeling and fervor. The letter to Mr. Stoddart, 1892, refers to his stories of rural life in Indiana: "Its romance is the romance of the crude, isolated and dreary existence of the farming people."

523. TRUMBULL, LYMAN AND YATES, RICHARD. A.L.S. by Trumbull. 8vo, 2pp. Alton, Ills. Nov. 8, 1856. With cabinet photograph signed. ✚Two carte-de-visite photographs of Yates autographed, and cut signature. Together five pieces.

Very fine Trumbull letter to W. P. Fessenden, describing the Buchanan campaign of 1856; mentioning Caton, Filmore, and ". . . we have routed the little Giant."

524. WALLACE, JOSEPH. A. MS. S. "Abraham Lincoln. A Study of His Style as a Writer and Speaker." 8vo, 21 pages. Springfield, Ill., June 1900. Tall 8vo, full black morocco, each page mounted.

Unpublished MS. by the author of a "Life of Col. Baker" and a "History of Illinois and Louisiana under French Rule." A.L.S. by H. E. Barker laid in.

525. WASHBURNE, E. B. ABRAHAM LINCOLN, His Personal History and Public Record. [Washington, 1860] 8vo, 4 leaves. Fish 1020. ✛THREE A.L.S. 1868, 1869, 1881.

526. WEIK, JESSE W. Lincoln's biographer. Two A.L.S. 4to, 2pp. Greencastle, Ind. March 30, 1895; and 4to, 1p. Oct. 18, 1896. Both to Maj. Lambert.

Two fine letters referring to a manuscript Weik had in preparation, "The Boyhood and Early Manhood of Lincoln . . . Lincoln used to say that a good many persons disapproved of dirty stories but he always noticed that no man ever left a room while one was being told . . ."

527. WELLES, GIDEON. Lincoln's Secretary of the Navy. THREE A.L.S. Two 4to, 1p. and one 8vo, 2pp. Washington 1863, 1864. Two cut signatures and engraved portrait laid in. Together six pieces.

528. WHITE, HORACE. Editor of The Chicago Tribune. FIVE A.L.S. 8vo, 7pp., 1865; 3pp., 1868 and 5pp. 1871 to Mr. Fessenden; 1p., 1891 to Hawley and 2pp., 1908 to J. S. Little.

529. WHITMAN, WALT. American poet. A. MS. Notes for his Scenes in War Hospitals. 4" x 10", circa 28 lines.

530. [WHITNEY, HENRY C.] Lincoln's law partner. TYPED MANUSCRIPT. "The 'Lost Speech.' (Unabridged)" 4to, 16pp. on Whitney's law office stationery.

The famous campaign speech delivered in Bloomington, May 29, 1856, which held the audience so spellbound on the subject of slavery in Nebraska, that no one copied it down. This is the text as Whitney recalled it, probably the nearest to the original available.

531. WOOD, FERNANDO. Copperhead politician. A.L.S. 4to, 3pp. Auburn, 1843. To Gov. W. H. Seward "Private." A.N.S., 2 cut signatures, engraving, and signature of C. L. Vallandigham. Together six pieces.

INDEX

To names not mentioned in the titles.

CHICAGO BOOK & ART AUCTIONS, INC.

SUITE 922 FINE ARTS BUILDING, 410 SOUTH MICHIGAN AVE., CHICAGO

Please buy for me at your AUCTION SALE No. _____*to be held on*_____*the following lots at not exceeding the prices named, which are* SO MUCH PER LOT, *each lot indicated by number. These bids are made subject to the conditions of sale printed in the catalogue of this sale. Persons not known to the firm are requested to furnish references or deposit.*

NAME_____

ADDRESS _____

_____   _____
         First Word   *First Word*

How to Bid by Mail

ATTENTION: Out-of-town buyers. Whether or not you are able to attend our sales in person we shall always be glad to execute your bids for you, purchasing at the lowest possible price in competition with the floor bidding. We regard your instructions as final and will bid in any manner you advise.

In order to bid on a lot in this catalogue read the descriptions carefully. Decide how much you are willing to pay for the lot. Put down on the bid sheet enclosed in this catalogue the price at which you expect to get the lot. Be sure to specify the maximum price you are willing to pay as we will not exceed your maximum, except, possibly, in the case of a tie between your bid and a bid from the floor when it may be necessary to exceed your bid 50c or $1.00 for you to break the tie.

Do not hesitate to bid whatever you like because of uncertainty as to the value of the material you desire. It is impossible to appraise rarities with any estimates that approach a nicety; and it is impossible to foretell what even important books will bring at public sales. Therefore we would advise you to send your bid according to your willingness to pay for a particular lot. All bids, whether for $1.00 or $1000.00, receive the same careful attention.

During the auction sales Mr. Meine himself handles all mail bids in competition with the bidding on the floor. If you have any special instructions which you would like to have Mr. Meine execute, he would be only too glad to do so. He devotes his entire time at the sale to seeing that out-of-town bids are properly executed.

Selling prices on lots lost by bidders will be reported free of charge if a self-addressed envelope is enclosed. We cannot, however, send out prices on lots which were not bid on. For this latter purpose we maintain a priced catalogue service of $1.00 per session. Bidders who have not established credit with us must furnish adequate Chicago references or send an advance deposit of 25% of the amount bid. This will be credited to your account and any balance remaining will be refunded after the sale.

CHICAGO BOOK & ART AUCTIONS, INC.

FRANKLIN J. MEINE, *Secretary and Manager*

Priced Catalogues

Copies of this catalogue marked with the prices realized at the sale may be obtained for two dollars, cash, with order.

This sale catalogue is of important bibliographical value to every Lincoln collector. Only a limited edition has been printed for the immediate needs of the sale.

In view of the significance of the sale and the heavy advance requests for catalogues, we recommend placing your order for a priced catalogue at once.

CHICAGO BOOK & ART AUCTIONS, INC.

410 SOUTH MICHIGAN AVENUE   CHICAGO, ILLINOIS

...Born ... ...
... near Charlotte Courthouse
Va - Kin
grandmother of A. Lincoln
called Lucy. Hanks ...
and Sparrow.

Nancy Lincoln mother
two Aunt? of Lucy Hanks
Houvain or Sparrow and
a son of Judge John Ma...
of Va.,

Nancy Hanks. Hon. ...
born near Lynchburg Va

Army Judge Marshall
killed in border warfare
Lincoln father only son
Judge Marsh... of Virginia
abraham I was Charlotte ...

CPSIA information can be obtained
at www.ICGtesting.com
Printed in the USA
BVHW040527201218
535872BV00025B/442/P

9 780483 291577